Living SANTERÍA

Rituals and Experiences in an Afro-Cuban Religion

Michael Atwood Mason

SMITHSONIAN INSTITUTION PRESS
Washington and London

© 2002 Smithsonian Institution
All rights reserved

Copy Editor: Gregory McNamee
Production Editor: Ruth G. Thomson

Library of Congress Cataloging-in-Publication Data
Mason, Michael Atwood.
     Living Santería : rituals and experiences in an Afro-Cuban religion / Michael Atwood
     Mason.
         p.   cm.
     Includes bibliographical references and index.
     ISBN 1-58834-052-X (alk. paper) — ISBN 1-58834-077-5 (paper : alk. paper)
         1. Santería. I. Title.
     BL2532.S3 M272002
     299'.674—dc21   2002021016

British Library Cataloging-in-Publication available

Manufactured in the United States of America
09 08 07 06 05 04 03 02 5 4 3 2 1

♾ The paper used in this publication meets the minimum requirements of the American
National Standard for Information Sciences—Permanence of Paper for Printed Library
Materials ANSI Z39.48-1984.

For David Brown, Katherine Hagedorn, and Ernesto Pichardo
—fellow travelers in this mad adventure

Turn loose the voices, undream the dreams. Through my writing, I try to express the magical reality, which I find at the core of the hideous reality of America.

In these countries, the [Afro-Cuban] god Elegguá carries death in the nape of his neck and life in his face. Every promise is a threat, every loss a discovery. Courage is born in fear, certainty of doubt. Dreams announce the possibility of another reality, and out of delirium emerges another kind of reason.

What it all comes down to is that we are the sum of our efforts to change who we are. Identity is no museum piece sitting stock-still in a display case, but rather the endlessly astonishing synthesis of the contradictions of everyday life.

I believe in that fugitive faith. It seems to me the only faith worthy of belief for its great likeness to the human animal, accursed yet holy, and to the mad adventure that is living in this world.

[Galeano 1991:125]

CONTENTS

ACKNOWLEDGMENTS

This adventure has been supported by many people who deserve special mention. From my parents I inherited both a passion for theology and religion that drives me and a pragmatism that sustains me.

At Indiana University, my research committee—especially Richard Bauman and Michael Jackson—provided me with guidance, encouragement, support, and freedom. Many administrators and support people at Indiana smoothed the way through numerous little glitches; my thanks to all of you. Several friends and colleagues made the time in Indiana more hospitable to me: Jana Giles, Sheila Guilfoyle, Soo Young Kim, Ona Kiser, Michael Nicklas, Jill Terry Rudy, George Schoemaker, and Rory Turner all listened to me talk through these ideas.

Ethnography, like all research, requires time and money. While at Indiana I received support from the Folklore Institute, African Studies Center, and the East Asian Studies Center. Summer fieldwork in 1990 in Washington, D.C., was supported by the District of Columbia Commission on the Arts and Humanities. My first field trip to Cuba was sponsored by the Cuban Studies Program at Johns Hopkins University's School of Advanced International Studies. Field trips in 1996, 1997, and 1998 were funded by the Smithsonian Institution's Office of the Provost and Scholarly Studies Committee. At the Smithsonian I have consistently received support in the form of time to work. Carolyn Margolis has been unwavering in her support. Through my work at "the Smith," many colleagues have discussed aspects of this book with me: Mary Jo Arnoldi, Mark Auslander, Linda Heywood, Jake Homiak, Adrienne Kaeppler, Ivan Karp, Christine Mullen Kreamer,

Robert Leopold, Marvette Pérez, Fath Ruffins, Sónia Silva, Theresa Singleton, Maria Sprehn Malagón, Barbara Stauffer, and John Thornton.

In Cuba, Rafael Leovigildo López Valdés and Enrique Sosa Rodríguez both befriended and guided me. Eusebio Leal Sprengler and the Office of the Historian of the City of Havana have facilitated my work on various occasions, as have Pedro Cosme Baños and the Municipal Museum of Regla. Other friends have made it possible to create the better part of a life in that relaxed and vivacious republic, which teeters between crisis and chaos: Antonio de Armas Arredondo, Elba Capote, Zoraida García, Alfonso García Cálves, Ana Margarita Gil Delgado, Betsy Hall, Walkiria López Pedroso and her daughter Gisela, the López-Sabina family, Ernesto Rey Palma and his family, Antonio Quevedo Herrero, Remberto Reymundo Chaguayceda, Orlando Rivero Valdés, Ivalú Rodríguez Gil, Roberto Rodríguez Menéndez, Milagros Vaillant, Ernesto Valdés Janet and his family, and Alberto Villareal.

Mi gente—my confidants—in the religion have accepted and taught me: Elia Cálves, Eugenia Cálves and her daughter Pancha, Raquel Fernández Vigil, Saúl Fernández and his extended family, Judith Gleason, Geraldo Nimo Quintana, Lourdes Pedroso Cálves and her son Juan Enrique, Norma Pedroso Cálves, Santiago Pedroso Cálves, and Humberto Pérez have been among the most important. All of you have added to this project, and I thank you. My thanks also go to fellow *santeros* here in Washington, D.C., who live with me in this community, and to those around the world who have guided me at different times. My appreciation and affection go to the people who have come to my house to seek the orichas. *Mo dupe o!*

David Brown, Katherine Hagedorn, and Ernesto Pichardo have been loyal and consistent interlocutors for years, and each has had a hand in forming my thinking and this text.

Beyond the human, other entities have facilitated the creation of this text. Elegguá, Olocun, and Ochún all carried me in different ways. The slow, careful, and indefatigable Obatalá proved to me that his proverb is true: Step by step you arrive far away—or in this case page by page. To them I say, *Maferefún Oricha*.

A version of chapter 1, "The Blood That Runs through the Veins," originally appeared in my master's thesis in folklore at Indiana University (1992) and later, with modifications, in *The Drama Review* (1993). A version of chapter 2, "I Bow My Head to the Ground," appeared in a special issue of the *Journal of American Folklore* (1994) dedicated to bodylore.

NOTE ON LANGUAGE AND ORTHOGRAPHY

In this book, non-English words are italicized on their first appearance (where they are usually defined), as well as when they are used as terms. Italicized words are identified as either Lucumí, the ritual dialect of the West African language Yoruba (see Olmstead 1953), or Spanish, the daily language spoken by most people who practice Santería. A few Yoruba words also appear. When a translation appears either in the text or in a parenthetical note, I have used abbreviations to indicate if the original word is Lucumí (Lu.), Spanish (Sp.), or a combination (Lu., Sp.). In some cases I have used an English translation of a common term and then provided the Lucumí and Spanish words in a parenthetical note.

Lucumí does not usually have plural markers for nouns; thus, *oricha* (Lu. deity) can be both singular and plural. However, it is also common to hear Lucumí words with Spanish endings; for example, *egun* (Lu. ancestral spirits) are sometimes called *egunes*. I have used these plural markers in most places for clarity. Similarly, because Lucumí is primarily an oral language with no standardized orthography, I have transcribed the words in their most common forms. These generally follow Spanish orthography but include the hard *k* and *w*. Although *s* and *z* produce the same sound and appear regularly in writing, I have consistently opted for *s*. The few Yoruba words that appear are very common and follow the common orthography, but I have deleted the subscript dot. Thus, *e* with a dot becomes a simple *e*, *o* with a dot becomes a simple *o*, and the *s* with a dot becomes *sh* for easy reading.

INTRODUCTION

Living Santería

In 1992 I underwent a ritual initiation to become a priest in Santería, an Afro-Cuban religion.[1] In deciding to do so, I changed my social life forever. I also changed the kind of ethnography that I could write about the religion. Because my social world now included intimate, lasting relationships with both people and spirits in Santería, my thinking and writing had to change. Not only was I responsible to academics in my own culture—colleagues in the American Anthropological Association, the American Folklore Society, and the Smithsonian Institution where I work—but I was also responsible to the followers of the religion, who are avid readers of any book written about their culture, and to the Cuban academy, which had sometimes welcomed me as one of its own. This responsibility to diverse readers underscores the performative aspect of research and writing, which involves various audiences, criteria for evaluation, and risks. It also underscores the common ritual and discursive nature of social life in both Santería and the academy. Self-fashioning can be and is accomplished by many means and in many domains (Greenblatt 1980).[2]

To respond to various audiences, I both employ and exploit the tenuous literary position of ethnography. Like many other cultural forms, ethnography appropriates and transforms other genres and forms to accomplish its aims (Bauman and Briggs 1990). In this ethnography I try to exploit the textuality of the writing, because ethnography will always be done in a genre, whether dissertation, monograph, or film, with generic expectations, limitations, and certain conventions and strategies (cf. Marcus and

Cushman 1982:31–46). It seems foolish to forgo the opportunities of the genre I have chosen.

The text moves between different voices. Field accounts and ritual descriptions lend themselves to a narrative voice, whereas more analytical sections call for more abstract language. The text's fluidity of perspective underscores and reiterates the symbolic and discursive nature of folkloristic and anthropological activities from participant-observation and formal interviews to the representation of other people as "evidence" for our theories (Domínguez 1991:15). The world described by an ethnography "is not the unmediated world of the 'other' but the world between ourselves and the others" (Hastrup 1992:117). This mediated world of the ethnographic encounter "defies our ordinary historical categories, and the field-world has neither a firm past nor a distinct future because its reality is intersubjectively constructed and depends on the ethnographer's presence in the field" (Hastrup 1992:127; cf. Fabian 1983). To reflect this interstitial world, to remind the reader that this ethnography does not simply reiterate the modernist paradigms, and to emphasize the vitality of lived experience, I have used the present tense throughout this text when describing rituals and other field experiences, just as I have woven narratives into descriptive and analytical passages. This symbolic, discursive approach to ethnographic writing fully implicates our language game— especially its tendencies to reify processes and then confer agency upon them.[3]

One such process is "writing culture," and ethnographers have employed many devices to represent authorship and to address the inherent subjectivity in their works. Authorship and the resultant authority provide the social "scientist" with claims to a positivistic, neutral, impersonal point of view (Okely 1992:9). Scientific authority borrows concepts, values, perspectives, and discourse from intellectual ancestors to represent other cultures and make knowledge claims about them. In so doing, it appropriates multiple voices (Bakhtin 1981), and it transforms the author into a function of discourse whose subjective and individual qualities are subsumed to the needs of the text (Foucault 1977:124).[4] However, this scientific stance obscures the realities of ethnographic practice, in which the ethnographer's subjectivity—body, capacities, identities, questions—enters into long-standing relationships with other subjects through which knowledge about their culture is revealed and shared, hidden and withheld. Ethnographers, like the people they encounter, are "multiple presences" of "infinite layers" and these differences—within individual ethnographers and between ethnographers and the people they work and live with—aid in the ongoing construction of identities (Trinh 1989:94, 104).

Because ethnography emerges from that interstitial and always social interaction between ethnographers and the people with whom they work, and because my experience as an ethnographer of Santería has been shaped extensively by my own identity, it seems important to discuss my involvement in the religion. It would be dishonest for me to write extensively about the creation of subjectivity and the constraints on agency in Santería and not to position myself clearly within the two dominant discourses that I engage and in which I seek competence (see Alcoff 1988). Since 1987 I have been exploring Santería with an intensely religious interest. My quest for knowledge began when I read about the transformative *oricha,* or deity, Oyá; I dreamed that I was invoking her and that she responded. In 1992, when all but my academic life was in ruins, I traveled to Cuba to undertake preliminary fieldwork and to undergo the initiation that would make me a priest of Ochún, goddess of rivers and love. When the gods spoke to me as part of my consecration, they spoke of a rebirth for me and of a duty to serve others through the religion. Since that time I have devoted at least one night a week to doing divination, making sacrifices, and staging various ceremonies for people in my community. This work peaked when I undertook a week-long initiation ceremony to consecrate a new priestess to Yemayá in 1996 and three others to various orichas in 1998.

After the last initiation, the new priestess and I were discussing the implications of surrendering our lives to service of the orichas, and in that conversation I had a flash of clarity: I explained that if I learned that I were going to die, I could accept it because I knew I had made a difference in people's lives. I knew I had helped at least four people transform their lives for the better. Serving the orichas has become as much a part of my life as being an academic or a member of my family.

Despite my involvement in the religion, this ethnography is not primarily a narrative of my experiences, although I do appear in it. This text has been shaped by my experiences as the object of ritual, my role as a performer of rituals, my colleagues and friends, and observations I have made over the last fifteen years. As I have struggled to find order in this overwhelmingly complex tradition, anthropological theory has helped me make sense of the religion. Similarly, my theorizing of my own religious practice keeps me connected to the culture into which I was born and in which I make part of my life.

INITIATION: MAKING *SANTO*

It is a hot Havana morning in July 1992. I have trouble staying awake. Last night the preparations lasted until well past midnight, and this morning the elders put me in a chair behind the door facing the wall. I cannot speak, eat, or move without permission from my godparents. The only exception has been when I stood with the others as we called the spirits of the ancestors to assist us and sang songs in Lucumí, the dialect of the West African language Yoruba used here as a liturgical language. These are the rules of the initiation as a priest in Santería, the most popular Afro-Cuban religious tradition.

My godmother brings me sweet, hot Cuban coffee that makes me cringe as I throw it back. The smell pervades the tiny apartment, but it does nothing to wake me up. I close my eyes and immediately begin to dream: I see a young Cuban woman standing in front of me and smiling warmly. We both begin to laugh. The sweetness of the moment reminds me of Ochún, the *oricha* (Lu. deity) of the river, beauty, and love. Through cowrie-shell divination, she has been identified as my deity, and it is to her that I am about to be consecrated, to "make *santo.*" She seems so close to me at this important moment.

The morning continues this way: I sit behind the door and yawn. The rhythmic chanting from the next room, the sacred precinct called the *igbodú* (Lu.), draws my attention, but the words are all in Lucumí. The rush of unfamiliar words leaves nothing to grab onto. I stare at the wall as I listen. I cannot stay awake. I close my eyes, only to be assailed by images of the deities, especially Ochún. Sometimes she is smiling, sometimes dancing, sometimes sitting by a river. Sometimes she wears the face of a friend, and I feel the undeniable weight of love.

After what seems like many hours, my godfather comes and stands next to me. He slips me some fried plantains, which I eat in a hurry. My godmother comes—all smiles—and gives me another shot of sweet, hot coffee. After I return the cup to her, I am again alone in the corner. I stare at the wall, and the many sounds in the apartment seem muffled. I doze off again but wake up as I feel cloth covering my head and falling around me. There is even more noise now, and I am told that I must close my eyes and keep them closed. Someone helps me stand and leads me to a door where I have to knock again and again.

From behind the door, a voice asks, "What are you looking for?"

"*Santo.* The saint."

"What santo?"

I hear my godfather near me saying, "Say 'Elegguá.'"

"Elegguá." This continues until I have named a host of divinities, ending with Ochún.

The door opens and I step inside the igbodú, where the elders have been working all morning. A man's voice tells me to put my bare feet together. Suddenly hot, wet blood covers the tops of my feet, and my eyes flash open for a second. The voice sings a short melody. A sweet smell reaches my nose, and I feel queasy. After a moment, I realize that they have sacrificed a bird over my feet. Then I am told to prostrate myself to my godmother. She helps me up and embraces me. I ask for her blessings, and she gives them.

For the next couple of hours, one thing happens right after another. I am told to kneel and my head is washed. Then I am told to stand, my clothes are cut off, and my body is washed. I am dressed again and told to stand in one place for a while. Then I am led to a place where I stand on a mat. Slowly they sit me down on a very hard stool. They plait the hair on the top of my head into a single braid.

Someone places cold metal scissors on my forehead, and my godmother begins to invoke all the spiritual powers of the universe: She asks for the blessings of Olofi, the High God. She asks for the blessings of the ancestors. She names one, then another, and then another. She asks for the blessings of the orichas and makes a long prayer to Ochún. Then she cuts off the braid. Many people repeat this process, each one invoking their ancestors and orichas before cutting away at my hair.

Then someone moves in with a straight razor as the elders start to sing again. The razor burns as it shaves away the stubble that remains on the crown of my head. The occasional nicks send out sharp pains. When this process is finished, they briefly place cool, fresh grated coconut on my head and take turns invoking the spirits and addressing my head. This time they paint the shaved area. I am not sure what they are painting, but each brush stroke is excruciating.

When this process ends, an old woman's voice asks for the blessings of God, the ancestors, and the orichas. She places something sticky on my head and addresses them asking for specific blessings for me: "With this *aché,* this sacred power, let him not see death, let him not see sickness, let him not see loss, let him not see wickedness. Instead give him health, give him luck, give him strength, give him tranquility, give him spiritual evolution."

The next priestess begins the same process. As soon as she begins to pray for me, I can take no more of this kindness. I begin to weep. I continue crying for several hours, as all the elders place the aché—powerful herbs that embody the deities—on my head. An old woman tries to comfort me, but my tears will not stop. More cloth goes over my head and the aché. I can feel that it is being suspended by people standing around me. The master of ceremonies crowns me first with the sacred objects of my godmother's orichas and then with my own. With each oricha, he invokes the powers and prays for my future and my well-being. By the time he crowns me with my godmother's Ochún, I am exhausted again—too much pain, too many tears, and too much weight on my head. Years of loneliness flow through me. Childhood memories of being beaten wash over me as strangers pray for me with incredible tenderness.

My Ochún crowns my head, and the head celebrant begins to sing to the orichas one after another. I can no longer stay awake. The first time I doze off, I am awakened by what feels like an electrical current starting on the top of my head and running down the sides. It feels as though an animal is burrowing into my head. I twitch several times, and the feeling intensifies as the celebrant and the elders sing more forcefully. This continues for a while, but then the singing stops. I twitch again. A hand goes to my shoulder, and an old woman says, "Okay, that's enough. Not now. Some other day. Ochún can come some other day."

Within Santería, the initiation ritual creating a lasting relationship between a person and an oricha is not an everyday occurrence, but it usually comes as part of a predictable trajectory that leads to greater commitment to and interaction with the orichas. Through this process many oricha worshipers begin as members of a ritual *ilé* (Lu. house) led by someone else only to end up as priestesses and priests leading their own communities in ceremonies to honor the spirits and orichas. After going for a consultation with a diviner, oricha worshipers are often asked to make sacrifices of various kinds. Working with herbs for physical healing or offerings for spiritual healing, followers of the orichas address a variety of circumstances. When indicated, they may also be asked to become initiated at different levels of commitment. The most common beginning is "receiving the necklaces" that symbolize the worshipers' connection to the orichas. The ceremony of "receiving the Warriors" provides oricha worshipers with sacred objects used to create and maintain a shrine for four protective deities. In priestly initiation, sacred objects and extensive revelation from the divinities provide the new priest or priestess with resources to begin to lead others into the religion.

In fact, the religion has developed a complex vocabulary to identify people with different levels of involvement with the spirits. The term *aleyo* (Lu. stranger) refers to a person who may attend ceremonies and turn to the orichas in times of crisis but who does not have any commitment to the religion. Both *omoricha* (Lu. children of the oricha) and *aboricha* (Lu. one who worships orichas) refer to all people who have some commitment and sustained relationship to the orichas[5]; these people may have received the necklaces or the protective warrior orichas. Among the omoricha are the *oloricha* (Lu. one belonging to the oricha); this title refers to anyone who has passed through the priestly initiation that connects his or her essence with the oricha. Oloricha act as priestesses and priests, guiding aleyos and other omoricha in their relationships with the orichas.

The orichas are differentiated in lavish detail, and each has distinct areas of influence in nature and human life. For example, Ochún wears yellow, uses gold and brass, and eats honey and hens; she "rules" love, female sexuality, sensuality, and the arts, and she lives in the river. Elegguá dresses in red and black, uses the simple tools of a farmworker, and takes rum and roosters; a trickster and messenger of the orichas, he rules communication, ritual power, male sexuality, and destiny, and he lives at crossroads and on the open savannah.[6]

Every person is believed to have a "head" oricha, and the physical head receives much attention in the complex rituals of the religion. First, the head, called *cabeza* (Sp.), *orí* (Lu.), or *eledá* (Lu.), is the spiritual faculty and central aspect of a human being. Before birth, each orí goes before the Creator and receives its essential character. This character, which people closely associate with an individual's destiny, can be either "hot" or "cool" (Cabrera 1980:121). Olorichas disagree about how mutable the head's character is, in part because the head also idiomatically refers to the oricha that rules a person; each individual establishes this relationship with a deity in front of the Creator before birth (cf. Bascom 1991:115).[7]

This central deity, often called "the owner of the head," represents an important part of the individual's character. For example, a child of the elegant and active oricha Ochún is usually thought to be extroverted, sensual, graceful, vivacious, and, some might say, flirtatious.[8] In fact, at times olorichas conflate the "owner of the head" and the individual; an "Ochún" refers to a child of Ochún who in ritual may act in the role of that oricha. The owner of the head can be identified through various divination systems, and a growing relationship between an individual and the owner of the head often leads to initiations, after which the *aché* (Lu.

power to accomplish; essence; herbal medicines) of the oricha literally resides inside the initiate's head; during and after priestly initiation, the oricha can "mount" the initiate in trance possession and thus take control of the body that they share.[9]

In possession, the oricha uses a human's body to dance, sing, salute ritual elders, purify the faithful, and give advice to members of the community. Through the sacrifice of various candles, objects, herbs, and food items, people placate and enlist the assistance of the spirits, whereas in divination they use traditional mechanisms such as coconut pieces, cowrie shells, or palm nuts to learn the disposition of the spirits and to determine what sacrifices will create the appropriate balance between the visible and invisible worlds.[10] By producing elaborate cultural rituals and ceremonies, Santería oloricha channel the aché—ritual generative power and authority—of the orichas.

Each oricha represents a different facet of the creator god, and so by worshiping the deities, people are worshiping the High God. The overarching god called Olodumare, Olofi, or Olorun established the order of the universe but is now essentially uninvolved in human affairs except before birth and after death. However, he left the universe in the hands of divinities called orichas or *santos* (Sp. saints). Along with these deities are ancestors and spirits of the dead called either *egun* (Lu.) or *espíritus* (Sp.). These various beings are constantly influencing people in this world, and the religion's many ceremonies focus human attention on them.

The basic elements of this theological and religious system arrived in Cuba with enslaved people. Of the ten to sixteen million people enslaved as part of the Atlantic slave trade, close to one million were brought to Cuba between 1511 and 1886. Although enslaved people were brought from many parts of Africa, a great plurality were from Yoruba-speaking areas of what are now Nigeria and Benin who arrived in Cuba in the last century of slavery (Moreno Fraginales 1977). These people brought with them the symbolically complex and philosophically subtle religious traditions that over time have been transformed into Santería or the Regla de Ocha (Lu., Sp. rule of the oricha).[11] Santería follows generalized notions of African religious structure,[12] but its practices were altered to fit the social circumstances of enslaved and free creole Cubans. The religion arrived in the United States with Cuban immigrants beginning in the 1940s. The Cuban Revolution of 1959 touched off the exodus of nearly a million Cubans, and these emigrants established the religion in the United States, Puerto Rico, Mexico, Colombia, and Venezuela. In each of these places, the Cuban-planted religion has taken root and grown dramatically. In the United States, it has flourished in large cities, embracing other Latinos and increasing numbers of African Americans and Euro-Americans.[13]

The historical experience of slavery and repression created an atmosphere of secrecy as the followers of the religion tried to protect themselves from the social forces that threatened them. Under slavery in colonial Cuba, the practice of the religion was technically illegal, and accusations of "witchcraft" could mean imprisonment or death. Although the exact conditions of the repression changed through time and certain domains existed where the religion flourished, both civil and Roman Catholic authorities routinely attacked the worship of the orichas (Ortiz 1984). In the republican era different regimes repressed the religion, and many senior priestesses and priests in Cuba still remember when their colleagues or elders had their altars destroyed and their most cherished religious objects literally cast into the street. In the years following the Cuban Revolution of 1959, the religion's "culture" was slowly valorized, and in the late 1980s the practice of the religion was decriminalized. However, many omoricha are still frightened about how their religion would be interpreted by the authorities should they get into trouble (see Hagedorn 1995, 2000, 2001). Similarly, immigrants to the United States have often hidden their involvement in the religion in an attempt to assimilate themselves into American society. Within the religion itself, secrecy also protects ritual knowledge and the power it implies. This ethos of secrecy plays an important role in the religion of the orichas among the Yoruba, as many ritual practices are secret and only accessible to initiated priestesses and priests (see Apter 1992; Matory 1993). Although these two types of secrecy—that of the immigrants and that of the Yoruba—have different origins, they function in much the same way: Santería is an essentially secret society, where most knowledge is guarded by those who have it.[14]

Some of the most closely guarded "secrets" allow competent olorichas to initiate new priestesses and priests. With time and training, someone at this level of initiation can start to guide others through this process and initiate them into the "mysteries of the orichas." In each of these ceremonies, the initiate receives stones and other objects through which he or she can communicate with the orichas, and each of these ceremonies channels aché, so that omoricha can experience the blessings of the religion: health, luck, strength, tranquility, and spiritual evolution.[15] These ceremonies are performed by ritual elders and place people into long-lasting relationships with orichas, thus permanently altering their social lives.

THEORIZING THE SUBJECT IN SANTERÍA

My involvement in the religion and my theoretical concerns with the inter-subjective relationships and experiences that generate ethnographic knowledge make it impossible for me to return simply to the tradition of the realist representation of the "Other" (see Fabian 1983). What follows, then, is not a straightforward exploration of the constructionist model of the self in Afro-Cuban cultural and social life (cf. Marcus 1991). Rather than focus on general notions of the person in the religion, I have focused more on the subjective experiences of those notions by individuals. This difference between the "moral person" of society and the "me" of an individual's experience represents a shift in emphasis from social structure to more personal meanings (Mauss 1938). Although Santería has standards for behavior and moral edicts, a focus on individual, lived experience is primary here.

Living Santería is always a social experience inasmuch as the individual is always in close contact with and under the influence of these other subjects, be they family members, orichas, or ancestors. However, the omoricha of Santería with whom I have been working and talking since 1987 conceive of each individual as having certain fixed qualities, talents, traits, and roles. These essential characteristics do not limit the individual's ability to change over time or in different circumstances but rather provide the context in which those changes take place. Because many experiences in the culture of Santería revolve around stabilizing, strengthening, and empowering the individual,[16] I have focused on questions of performance as social action and have directed my attention toward issues of ethos, tone, and flavor in ethnographic inquiry.

This ethnography presents the lived experience of specific individuals in Santería as they use rituals to create, negotiate, and transform key relationships with elders, ancestors, and divinities. These people believe that each individual has specific talents and weaknesses as well as a unique destiny, and that destiny has brought them for whatever reason into the religion of the orichas. Destiny is often referred to as a road (Sp. *camino*), and many rituals use this important image and idea to explore the existentially precarious movement of human subjects through the world.[17] The image of the road suggests a lack of stability and need for movement in the life of each individual, and this motion sometimes conflicts with people's notion of order; as the philosopher Gabriel Marcel points out, "Perhaps a stable order can only be established if man [*sic*] is acutely aware of his condition as a traveler, that is to say, if he perpetually reminds himself that he is required to cut himself a dangerous path across the unsteady blocks of the universe. . . . This path leads to a world more firmly established in Being, a world whose changing and uncertain gleams are all that we can discern here below" (Marcel 1962:153–154). These words could easily come from the mouth of an eloquent *santero* (Sp. priest of Santería) trying to explain the experience of a lifeworld filled with powerful supernatural beings and ambitious humans, each with a predestined road. In their social fields, spirits of the dead and orichas hold key positions in the hierarchy and are treated essentially as specific kinds of "moral persons" with culturally appropriate and particular capacities, responsibilities, and needs; they fulfill their social roles in predictable ways (Mauss 1938). Gaining the help and following the advice of these supernatural beings through ritual allows humans to change their destiny. These rituals figure prominently in people's accounts of their lives: they become extraordinary experiences that help define the past, present, and future (Abrahams 1986b). Any account of the person in the Regla de Ocha must address this continuum of personhood that includes humans, active ancestral spirits, and the orichas—and the experience of life in this world.

To address the very real multiplicity of the lived experience of human persons and to include the spirits and gods in my discussion, I have adopted the term *subject*,[18] by which I mean any actor in the social field whose presence is constituted and sustained through ongoing social processes.[19] This subject includes various notions of power, autonomy, and interdependence, their social and bodily capacities, as well as the consciousnesses, selves, and identities that each subject experiences, creates, and transforms.[20] Thus the construction of subjectivity—the focus of this book—includes all subjects who influence the practices of Santería, from the uninitiated who participate in certain ceremonies and the police who interrupt them to the ancestors and orichas who are the focus of these activities. In this discussion the term *person* applies only to human beings when they are not fully possessed by other subjects.

This book explores the lived experience of various human subjects at different levels of involvement in the tradition. The chapters track the changing nature of subjectivity as an individual deepens social relationships with the spirits and elders in the religion. Together the chapters explore experiences that are common to most practitioners as they enter the tradition; the book begins as an outsider seeks the spirits' assistance, explores various changes in relationships with the spirits and the elders, and ends with the challenges faced by priests as they urge the spirits to act in the social world.

The first chapter of the book, "'The Blood That Runs through the Veins': Defining Identity and Experience in Dilogún Divination," focuses on the evocation and discussion of a complex, personal identity in a cowrie shell divination ritual (Lu. *dilogún*). Through verbal exchange with the client, the diviner reiterates what the orichas say and indexes a wide array of the client's social experiences in the ritual. Through proverbs suggested by the divination, the diviner explores difficulties in the client's emotional life and family circumstances. The tensions presented do not resolve, but the diviner simply elaborates them and juxtaposes them with the tensions that exist between the client and the orichas. The client experiences many different identifications and recalls a series of difficulties in a short period, and only sacrifice to the orichas promises any remedy.

Engaging the growing scholarship on the emergent meanings and uses of the body in ritual, the second chapter, "'I Bow My Head to the Ground': Creating Bodily Experience through Initiation," explores how the preliminary initiation of the *Guerreros* (Sp. Warriors) teaches the neophyte new bodily patterns. The formal gestures executed by the initiate's body show membership in and commitment to the religious community. The meaning of the gestures lies not so much in abstract formulations and concepts but in their performance within the ritual context. Much of the ritual focuses on preparing and cleansing the head of the initiate, who then participates in an animal sacrifice and must assume certain body positions. The ritual ends when the neophyte prostrates himself in front of the initiators in a bodily demonstration of respect.

However, practitioners negotiate their respect for their ritual elders and commitment to the religion with other interests. The third chapter, "'My Pants Are Bloody': Negotiating Identity in American Santería," focuses on the many relationships and social roles that a single individual must negotiate. Here the lived experience of individuals and their subjective values and interpretations come to the fore. The practice of the religion influences most aspects of a practitioner's life, but the effects are complex and nuanced. Personal history and ethnicity create a set of expectations about what is appropriate and when, and the religion may or may not conflict with those expectations. Practitioners often ignore or subvert the expectations of their employers by observing religious practices in the workplace. The religious community also enforces strict rules pertaining to appropriate interactions between people and the supernatural world. In each case, the individual strives to perform according to the expectations of the most important human observers as well as those of the ever-present supernatural ones.

The fourth chapter, "Living with the Orichas: Ritual and the Social Construction of the Deities," explores how the social reality of the supernaturals is created through the initiation of a new priestess or priest. This chapter explores the presence of the orichas as it is constituted in the *asiento* (Sp.) or *kariocha* (Lu.), the most highly marked ritual in the religion in which a person is consecrated as a priest or priestess of the orichas. The gods "rule" an assortment of geographical features, herbs, weather patterns, colors, animals, and actions; they also dwell in the sacred objects—stones and cowrie shells—that are consecrated with a new santero. All these features, which embody the presence of the orichas, are brought together in the asiento. For example, the initiate may visit the places that are associated with her central oricha. Herbs of that oricha are used to wash the initiate and the sacred stones she will receive; some of these herbs are powdered and placed in incisions on the shaved head of the initiate. Those same stones are placed on the shaven head of the initiate and later "eat" the favorite animals of the orichas through blood sacrifice. Multiple incarnations of the oricha are brought to bear in the ritual, and many touch the initiate. At this point, the oricha often takes possession of the new santero, and for a moment the oricha and the initiate are one. At the end of this ritual the initiate also receives a new name that is a praise name of the central oricha. Now the initiate is called by the oricha's name, and a "connective" relationship between them has been fully cemented. In the asiento, the oricha's presence is gathered and transferred to the initiate. The new *santera* (Sp. priestess) will represent the oricha in certain situations as well as act as an advocate for that spirit oricha.

"Imagining Power: The Aesthetics of Aché in Santería," the fifth chapter, explores how people in different positions within the religion imagine ritual and social power differently. The sources and nature of aché vary with the person who explains them, but certain patterns emerge along gender lines. Male practitioners usually describe power as emerging from the possession and deployment of esoteric knowledge (Sp. *conocimiento*) appropriate to the situation. Women usually discuss the connection between aché, faith, and a good heart; for them, the sentiment (Sp. *sentimiento*) that a person puts into a ritual situation determines its outcome, and they extol generosity and reciprocity in relationships. Certainly, these different explanations reproduce Cuban stereotypes about gender, but they also produce different strategies in the religious context. However, other factors mitigate these different strategies. In the asiento, every priest and priestess receives an *itá* (Lu. history) in which each oricha received speaks directly to the initiate about the difficulties and blessings to be expected as well as certain stories and proverbs that can be used as guides through the challenges of life. As initiates use these resources, the proverbs become generative schemata that give coherence to their experiences and structure their actions. If followed carefully, these cultural resources help create a successful, moral, individualized person.

As I said, I have chosen to focus on these ritual moments because they show various people at different levels of engagement with the religion's spirits. These rituals not only show the changing nature of subjectivity—a matter taken up in the sixth and final chapter, "Santería and the Social Construction of Subjectivity"—but they also follow a relatively common trajectory of deepening involvement with the ancestors and the orichas. For many people, a divination ritual provides their first real introduction to the tradition. Here the client is essentially an object of ritual, simply answering questions and listening passively as the diviner describes the current nature of the relationship between the client and the spirits. In contrast, an initiated priestess uses her notions of generative power to decide when and how to perform ceremonies. She is a full subject, aware of various identities and capacities, identified deeply with the spirits, and able to perform the verbal and bodily gestures necessary to move them into action. At each specific moment the rituals constitute and act upon the relationships between people and the spirits: through words and bodily actions, as objects and as subjects of those words and actions, through juxtaposition and identification with the spirits. The lived experience of Santería practitioners can be understood only when these practitioners are recognized and represented as complex experiencing subjects who are richly nuanced with bodily capacities as well as competing multiple ideological allegiances and identities, all of which are webbed together reflexively and unreflexively in idiosyncratic yet patterned ways.

"THE BLOOD THAT RUNS THROUGH THE VEINS"

Defining Identity and Experience in Dilogún Divination

María cannot sleep at night. It is May 1990, and it is unbearably hot. She is restless, nervous. Her eyes dart about searching the darkness for a clue to her discomfort. She is about to leave town, about to move back to her mother's house after being away for six years. She realizes that she needs help and, early the next morning, calls me. I make an appointment for her to consult an *oríaté* (Lu.), a diviner and priest in the Afro-Cuban religious tradition called the Regla de Ocha.

When we arrive at the diviner's house outside Washington, D.C., María rings the bell for the upstairs apartment. A small Cuban woman lets us in, explaining that her husband, the oríaté, is still in the shower. Together we climb the stairs. We are asked to sit with a newborn baby while a television broadcasts professional wrestling. At the left corner of the far wall, María sees the shrine to the oricha, the deities of the Regla de Ocha. My friend asks me to explain what we see.

Two bookcases stand side by side, one for the woman who answered the door and one for the oríaté; on the shelves are soup tureens in various colors. These tureens contain the sacred stones, or *otanes* (Lu.), physical manifestations of the oricha. Symbols for each oricha surround the tureens: There is Obatalá's white horse-tail switch, a traditional African symbol of authority, perfect for the senior oricha. The bookcase in the corner has a large blue and white tureen on top, with blue carnations next to it: this tureen is for Yemayá, mother of the oricha and ruler of the sea. There is Oyá's black horse-tail switch for the oricha associated with the dead—and with it, her copper crown and nine tools. There is the *batea Changó*, a covered wooden bowl that rests on top of an overturned wooden mortar; Changó is the majestic king. The tureens all have food around them. Yellow pastries are for Ochún, the flowing goddess of rivers and love. The watermelon at the base of the bookcase is for Yemayá. In the right corner stands a small, low table covered with white cloth and containers of water; this is the *bóveda* (Sp.), the shrine of the dead, and next to it rest several dolls to represent important ancestral spirits.

After a while, the oríaté appears from the back of the apartment, and the woman and I follow him into the kitchen. Seated at a table, the diviner has in front of him a small, flat reed basket; on the basket lie twenty-one cowrie shells, with their rounded side removed so they can fall face-up or face-down. There are also some hard candies and a small red and black clay figure. This is Elegguá Echú Oníkokó, the god of speech and the knower of destiny. As he prepares the table, the diviner asks María if she and I are married.

"No," she responds.

"*¿Hermanos?*" (Sp. siblings) counters the diviner.

"No."

"Oh, just friends," he says, laughing. In fact, we have been friends since we met as college freshmen six years before.

The oríaté begins to chant prayers in Lucumí, a dialect of Yoruba that is used as a liturgical language in Ocha. As he prays, he dips his fingers into a small glass of water and dribbles it on Elegguá and on the shells, another manifestation of the oricha. After this, he rubs sixteen shells together in his hands and then in small circles on the basket. He holds the shells to María's forehead and shoulders. After finishing this procedure, the oríaté raps on the basket three times, for three is the sacred number associated with Elegguá. He drops the shells and counts those that land with their serrated "mouths" up. Five. Oché is the name of this *odu* (Lu.), or divination figure. "Maferefún Ochún. Thanks be to Ochún. Oché speaks of the blood that runs through the veins (Sp. *la sangre que corre por las venas*) and you must protect everything inside, do you understand me?" He gathers the cowries again and again drops them. Eleven cowries land with their mouths up; Ojuani is the figure through which San Lázaro speaks. It portends much danger. Again the diviner describes the specific situation, but now he is focusing on the entire double-figure, Oché-Ojuani. He uses proverbs, gives advice, and asks more questions about the woman's social situation. She responds to all his inquiries, elaborating on the details of her life.

The oríaté again raps on the table three times. "Iré, Elegguá?" "Does the figure carry good luck, Elegguá?" Oché. He throws again to clarify. Oché again. He explains that Oché Meyi, as this figure is called, is the only figure to carry luck here; the woman is very lucky and the diviner seems amazed. He interprets this figure in the same manner as before. Proverbs, advice, questions, stories. The process repeats as the diviner discovers what kind of good luck the woman has. He asks about her family; she responds that she is about to return to her mother's house, which is torn by anguish. The mother has recently broken up with a long-time lover; the sister has recently tried to commit suicide; the woman is troubled by her feelings and cannot seem to find a solution to her problems. The oríaté finds out which oricha will help the woman and what sacrifice should be offered. Each time he throws the shells, he has new advice and new questions for the woman. With each throw she relaxes a little more.[1]

María is troubled; even if she is just trying to learn more about herself, at some level she is in crisis. The divination ritual helps clarify her position in the social and supernatural worlds. After her situation is clarified, she is able to act, to make a sacrifice that plants her squarely in the larger cosmological context. The ritual of dilogún divination touches on a multitude of experiences within the client's life, evoking various social identities she maintains. It juxtaposes these experiences with a single, clear course of action that promises to redress the various challenges she faces in her life.

My goal here is to understand one aspect of the subjectivity of the client. In using a phenomenological approach that allows the field experience as data to speak to me (Jackson 1989:4), the event under study becomes enmeshed in my own vision of the other people involved in the field experience. We experience the divination together (Devereux 1967:20), and the meanings emerge from that shared experience (Bauman 1977; Williams 1973:11).

This shared experience, however, cannot be fully communicated in language. Experience, as lived by real people, never fits perfectly into categories of thought or anthropological and folkloric models; experience overflows the concepts used to describe and understand it (Sartre 1969:49). Similarly, the experience of another person is always inaccessible. We cannot completely know the experience of another person; we can only understand the expressions of their experience (Crapanzano 1980:xi), the symbols used to represent life. These idioms exist in different genres, and I have tried to gather as many representations of divination experiences as possible. I have been "read" by the dilogún, have interviewed many diviners as well as other people who have been read, and have watched the process repeatedly. This involvement leads to a double goal: to present divination in a way that fits with these various commentaries by friends and informants and to present it in a way that resonates with my own understanding of the tradition and experience.

The interior world of the client (Sp. *cliente*), almost invisible to the diviner's eyes, troubles her and presents danger. From the beginning of the *consulta* (Sp. consultation), the client's inner world needs attention. Her own emotional and social position becomes the focus of the consulta, which reveals the present crisis, its supernatural solution, and the destiny of the client (Brandon 1983:222; Cabrera 1980:179; Sánchez 1978:43). Destiny, as construed in the Regla de Ocha, occupies an important space and encompasses all past actions, present troubles, and future possibilities (Cabrera 1980:197). The cowrie shells and the diviner confront the client with her own experience.

Divination apparently reduces anxiety and provides a basis for action. This is a truism. But the method by which divination clarifies situations and offers solutions remains unclear. In this case the figure, the single fall of the shells (Velásquez 1990b), implies a specific proverb that the diviner and then María can employ as an essential and inexhaustible interpretive frame for the problem at hand. Despite some variation in the Regla de Ocha, Oché regularly evokes "the blood that runs through the veins."[2] Advice follows the proverb and accompanies the rhetorical question, "Do you understand me?" By mixing the figure-specific proverbs and advice, the diviner supplies the client with a way to imagine and understand her situation.

With each throw the woman relaxes a little. The diviner again gathers the shells. Eleven. Oché-Juani. He asks about troubles with the police; María says no, no problems with the police. The diviner continues to explain that she must guard against troubles with the police. She resists this idea and seems detached from what is happening, amused and almost uninvolved. He says that it could be someone in the family.

"Are there problems with your family?"

The questions begin by exploring María's personal situation and experience of daily life. The questions asked of the client in this specific consulta reveal the common concerns and crises that compel people to visit the diviner. The interior—her body, her emotions, thoughts, and spiritual concerns—

surfaces almost immediately and becomes a central context and concern of the session. Is she healthy? Has she visited a doctor? Has she been ill? Is she worried? Always thinking about today's business? And tomorrow's?

The next questions relate María to the larger society. Frequently, it seems, members of the Cuban-American community interact with the police and the court system.[3] Putting aside the causes of this interesting and disturbing phenomenon, it is important to notice this concern with the more institutionalized parts of American culture. Is there trouble with the police? Are you in trouble with the law? The figure Oché-Juani suggests being caught at something, being trapped. When María replies with surprise and hesitates to agree, the diviner suggests that perhaps it is someone in the family; this connection of the individual to her social surroundings implies a sense of self different from that of Euro-Americans. The boundaries of the self are not limited to the individual but also encompass the family and political environment. The troubles that bring the client to the orichas may be a problem in her own life or a problem in the life of a family member; a problem in the family creates a problem for the individual.

After María hesitates again, the oríaté asks, "Have you had problems with your family?" Attention now bears on the family itself. María quickly says that she does not have problems but her sister has been troubled *("yo no tengo problemas, pero hay problemas con mi hermana")*. The details of the trouble are revealed: María's sister has been fighting with her mother. A problem emerges as significant and disturbing to the client.

"The blood that runs through the veins" is mapped onto different levels of the client's life. Oché-Juani suggests that there is a problem somewhere, and, in fact, few people visit a diviner unless a problem exists. The blood can be the literal blood of the client; the relationships within a family can also be construed as its life, its blood. The life of the body, the family, and the whole society merge in the proverb. The visual part of the metaphor—the blood coursing through the veins—unites the different realms of potential crisis: "Pictorializing in this way we can inspect the organizing images that are at play in ritual performance and see how microcosm and macrocosm, inner things and outer things, centers and peripheries, upper things and lower things, time-present and time-past are related. For out of such parts are wholes constructed" (Fernandez 1986:165). The image applies to each area of life—the body, the family, the polity, and relationships with the orichas—and further exploration through cowrie shell divination offers a solution to the problem. The metaphor, which emerges from the extraordinarily diverse choices possible in cowrie divination, is activated by the fall of the sign Oché and becomes meaningful and useful in comprehending the immediate circumstances (Jackson 1989:144). Thus a three-sided dialectic begins: The orichas, through their shell "mouths," direct the oríaté to explore specific contours of the problematic situation, and María responds positively and negatively until a consensus emerges. For María to be at peace, to be in balanced relationships, and to live productively, her blood must run smoothly through her many veins.[4]

The problems at hand, the lack of money, the appearance and sense of failure as she returns home, and the anxiety of that return—all these elements create stress. María changes her normal behavior and seeks out a different community in which to find answers, to develop solutions; a breach of normalcy occurs (Turner 1988:74). She leaves the English-speaking world in which she usually lives and works and finds an alternative community that, at least to some extent, resembles the Puerto Rican society of her mother's family. The crisis continues as she struggles for clarity and a path of action. María performs a social drama with a cast of one (Turner 1988:74–75), although not completely alone because I accompany her. She frames this event as meaningful and important; several facts evidence the importance of the ritual to her. At a time when she struggles financially, she pays the diviner a ritual fee (Sp. *derecho*) of twenty-five dollars; this money represents an important investment, for it could have been used to buy something more physically essential. At the end of the day, after returning from the bookstore where she holds a part-time job to augment the income of her full-time job as an editor for a non-profit organization, María discussed the consulta at length with me and recorded much of it in her journal; she also requested that I make a copy of the field tape for her so she could review the reading later. The monetary sacrifice and the desire to consider the reading repeatedly and in detail indicates its import as part of a larger drama in María's life, and that it is an "extraordinary experience" for her (Abrahams 1986a, 1986b:60; Dewey 1934:35). She explains, "I enjoyed what he said about me, you know, I like participating in things like that. . . . I, I just took it as an opportunity to learn more about myself" (Hernández 1991).

"Are there problems in your family?" asks the oríaté.
"I don't have problems, but there are problems with my sister."
"Problems she has had with, with your mother?"
"Yes. They fight a lot."
"Are you married?" he asks.

"No," she responds quickly.
"Do you have a boyfriend?"
"No," again quickly.
"Have you had one?"
"I used to have one."

Through many questions, the diviner asks María to tell him things about herself. She responds quickly and, in general, candidly. When asked about problems with the law, she laughs. When asked about troubles in the family, she answers the question and adds useful and pertinent information. The questions and answers, as is already evident, significantly add to the ritual (cf. Fitzgerald 1975:227); the diviner blends the information that he sees in the sign of the shells with what the client reveals (Velásquez 1990b).

These questions offer, in the course of the consulta, an opportunity for self-revelation. Frequently a person volunteers not just a bit of helpful information, as María does, but whole narratives about the troubling situation (Brandon 1983:239–240); if the diviner hits on a relevant concern, the client can expose more or less information about the circumstances, can externalize as much or as little of her interior self as she chooses. When asked if she has visited a doctor, María responds that she has not, and she then asks if the problems with *"lo interior"* (Sp. the interior) are "physical or mental or emotional or spiritual" (Velásquez 1990a); she asks the oríaté to clarify the idea of the interior as she attempts to understand better its importance and meaning.

Although many people reveal the details of their personal lives in response to the diviner's questions, no one is required to say anything. Commonly, a person gives no clarification of his reasons for coming to the diviner; the client whispers a question to the shells, and thus the diviner cannot manipulate the client (Bascom 1980:5, 1991:68–69; Brandon 1983:230; Sánchez 1978:53). Still, even in the extreme case where the client refuses to aid the diviner, questions are answered.

In my fieldwork, as I said, I have had many consultas with the cowries. I have tried different strategies to see what effect, if any, they had on the readings.[5] I have had readings in which I spoke little after each question; in others I provided only the information requested, only answered the questions; in still others I used the questions as opportunities to speak candidly and at length about my concerns and feelings. Each degree of participation produced readings with a distinct character. When I revealed only what was asked directly, the readings were brief and laborious; essentially the diviner defined my experience solely by what the shells suggested. Here I had to restrain myself from speaking; it seemed as though the oríaté were arbitrarily defining my situation as I struggled silently to evaluate whether his definition fit my experience. When I offered detailed accounts of important issues in my life, the readings left me feeling renewed, refreshed, and with a sense of having revealed myself[6]; these readings seem to flow naturally. Despite the differing tones, however, it is important to remember that in each case the structure of the ritual remained the same and it was my experience that changed; not only did the ritual structure my experience,[7] but it also provided options for different kinds of experience.

These different kinds of involvement and experience within the ritual structure suggest that the person being "searched" (Sp. *registrado*) can experience what I will call "reflective flow." In the literature on experience, authors commonly posit a dichotomous and dialectical relationship between reflection about experiences on the one hand and uninterpreted, uninterrupted experience on the other (see Csikszentmihaly and Robinson 1990; Abrahams 1986b:50–53; Jackson 1989:13; V. Turner 1986:42, 1988:86).[8] In many situations, especially in ritual, there exists a kind of experience that is equally reflective and fluid. In the consulta, the client is objectified and her life is defined and narrated by the oríaté, creating an intense sense of self-consciousness (Abrahams 1986b:56), but actions and responses to questions still occur in a natural and comfortable way. Here reflexivity and flow are simultaneous as María answers questions about herself; she "restores behavior" as she narrates a different and more detailed version of her life (Schechner 1985:35). Although her presentation of self occurs in the discontinuous format of questions and answers, she performs her life in a comfortable, fluid manner. Of central importance here is the role of ritual. Erving Goffman presents a valuable vision of ritual: "In brief, a play keys life, a ceremonial keys an event. . . . Once it is seen that ceremonials have a consequence that scripted dramas and even contest do not, it is necessary to admit that the engrossment and awe generated by these occasions vary greatly among participants" (1974:58). Although in a given ritual or ceremony not all the participants have the same experiences, I am arguing for the possibility that some people will experience reflective flow, where they are hyperconscious of their actions and still not self-consciously awkward.[9]

But as María answers the oríaté's questions and performs herself, she also reveals the fundamental diversity of her own experiences. In the example that opens this section, she comments about many things in a short time; the exchange takes place in about four seconds. Despite its brevity, the exchange uncovers many aspects of her life. First, she positions herself socially; she is neither married nor does she have a boyfriend. The fact that she has had a boyfriend indexes her sexual tendencies; she is either bisexual or heterosexual. This exchange also contrasts two specific times in María's life. She responds, "I used to have one [a boyfriend]"; this period of her life, of her past, contrasts with the present when she lacks that kind of companionship and intimacy. More generally, this issue of the past and present is especially important to Cuban Americans living in exile who make up the vast majority of practitioners of Ocha in the United States; the present in the United States often contrasts drastically with the past in Cuba.

Other questions index other aspects of her life. The questions about her family again touch on social relationships, and she states that she has a sister, that her mother is alive, and the two of them do not always get along. Her position in her family appears as central to the reading. At another moment, when the oríaté gives her advice, she assents to the fact that she is constantly worried about the future, that she is troubled inside. The diviner "said some things that I think are true about my personality" (Hernández 1991).

She reveals herself as a "multiple presence" of "infinite layers" (Trinh 1989:94): past and present, social life internalized and externalized. These differences, all part of María's life, do not annul identity but aid in its creation (Trinh 1989:104); her experience of herself includes all these times and relationships, not to mention the feelings that she has about them, and it is precisely these remembered historical moments and specific relationships that make her most naturally and completely herself (Abrahams 1986b:56). Like Gayatri Spivak (1990:38), "I do not intend a simplistic definition of identity"; instead I offer questions about the "experiencing subject" (see Bruner 1986:9).

An experiencing subject can be seen as a function of social relationships. Individuals are equated with their social roles. María is a *woman*, a *writer*, a *lover*, a *daughter*, and a *Puerto Rican American* whose father is from the northwestern United States and whose mother is from Puerto Rico. Each of these social positions has traditional behavior attached to it (cf. Dundes 1980); she is none of these things in isolation. Yet, paradoxically, María is all these things at once. Similarly, she fits into many rhetorical positions; she is *I* when speaking and *you* when addressed (Lacan 1978:298); she occupies no singular position in social life or discourse. Still her identity and subjectivity can be seen "as an emergent property of historicized experience" (Alcoff 1988:431). Thus, María as an experiencing subject exists in a specific historical context that acts as a frame and helps create meaning. She experiences herself and the events of her life through all these lenses.

"The 'self' cannot, therefore, be treated as a thing among things; it is a function of our involvement with others in a world of diverse and ever-altering interests and situations," writes Michael Jackson (1989:3). Social roles and groups frame what people experience and thus give their experiences specific kinds of meaning, but this meaning is never final, exclusive, or determinate. Yet neither María nor her experience can be reduced to these facts of social life; she is more than the sum total of her social positions. I have tried here to describe both general experiences of divination and those specific to her.

The oríaté discovers which oricha will help the woman and the sacrifice that should be offered. Ochún, the ruler of the sign Oché, will help María. "Acuaró [Lu.], Ochún?" (A sacrifice of partridges, Ochún?) Six followed by seven shells. Obara-Odí. Here the diviner uses the shells to provide a simple yes-or-no answer, and he does not explore the other meanings of the sign. Yes, a sacrifice of two partridges will clear the road.

With each throw María relaxes a little. The shells tell her that Ochún, who rules "sweet" water, honey, love, passion, and *lo interior,* will come to her aid; to gain this assistance, María must make an *ebó* (Lu. sacrifice) to Yalorde (Lu. a praise-name for Ochún). The sacrifice will reestablish the balance between the supernatural world and the human world; this lack of balance between the worlds causes the troubles. The act of sacrifice, then, becomes an essential moral act. To sacrifice is to create balance and evoke healing; after sacrificing to Ochún, María is more likely to receive her help and call on her in the future. Thus, the establishment and maintenance of relationships with the orichas represents an important part of destiny, as construed by members of the Regla de Ocha.[10]

As a point of contact between these two domains, the sacrifice acts to unite the two. Divination and the subsequent sacrifices often objectify the immediate and subjective situation, recast it in a large, mythological context, and provide a route for action (Jackson 1989:66), but my interest here is the method of the recasting. As I have already made clear, the various parts of the client's subjectivity come to the fore during a consulta de dilogún. Rather than attempt to simplify any singular problem, the reading records a series of conflicts and tensions within the client. Although predominantly verbal, the ritual orchestrates different kinds of experience to intensify the crisis (Kapferer 1986:194). Here the divination figures evoke or "contain," as the diviners say, certain proverbs. These proverbs lead to questions that personalize the situation and involve the client in the reading; also contained in the figures are stories of mythical characters and their troubles. Advice culled from the proverbs and stories instructs the client how to live, what to do and what not to do, how to interact with the family, and how to win the help of the orichas. Each turn represents a subtle variation in the theme at hand. The blood that runs in the veins can be any kind of internal problem, but each question intensifies the issues, even if it only provides an example of what the client is not experiencing. Although the problems that plague the client are not solved—that is, there is no guarantee that María's sister and mother will stop fighting and that María will stop worrying—the reading intensifies the situation.

Within the religion's definition of the situation, the cause of the problems frequently lies in some imbalance between the supernatural and human worlds. After this intensification of the realities of life, the diviner offers a method to transcend the situation. "Ochún wants partridges," he tells her. Each oricha has particular foods: Ochún is partial to hens, fish, partridge, eggs, shrimp, oranges, and fine pastries. The conflicts are further intensified by the deity wanting something. Not only is María worried about her family and her finances, but she now also has to concern herself with the demands of the goddess. These demands are numbered along with her other concerns but carry a different weight. This problem can be solved: a sacrifice to Ochún.

The diviner carefully evokes the problems of the client but does not solve them. In reality he cannot solve her problems, nor can he make her stop worrying. The issues remain in their original tension but are more explicit and are now juxtaposed with the new problem. This intensification and clarification forces the client to identify more and more with the reality of the situation (see Lévi-Strauss 1979:321, 323). The sacrifice, a method to solve one problem, becomes a catharsis for all the tensions discussed during the consulta.[11] The next chapter explores a larger sacrifice and how it teaches a new set of body patterns and practical actions within the religion.

With each throw the woman relaxes a little. Because she lacks the time and money to return to the oríaté and sacrifice the partridges, she goes to a river, the home of Ochún, and offers five yellow candles, five oranges, and five chocolate chip cookies.[12] Only time will tell if her devotion will change the destructive dynamics at play or if her improvised sacrifice intensified the conflicts in her situation and released some of the tension. And only time will tell if her improvised sacrifice will be enough to please Ochún.

"I BOW MY HEAD TO THE GROUND"

Creating Bodily Experience through Initiation

Bright light shines from the next room, and music pours into the dark living room where a young Euro-American sits alone. As he waits, he watches the pattern of the blinking Christmas lights in his godmother's suburban Maryland home. A 1990 calendar advertises Botánica San Lázaro, which his godmother, Idaberta, owns and manages. George Carter knows that the songs honor the orichas that constitute the pantheon of Santería[1]; his *padrinos* (Sp. godparents) are creating the sacred herbal water, *osain* (Lu.). Soon they will use it to cleanse him and baptize the divinities that he is to receive. He is separated because only the fully initiated can witness the making of the osain. As a new godchild of the same house, I sit with him and wait.

He is called into the room and kneels over a large basin in the middle of the floor. I too am called in and watch as the ceremony unfolds. He hangs his neck on the edge of the basin and water pours over his head. "Get his neck," says a voice from behind him; his godfather, José, splashes the liquid onto the man's neck and rubs vigorously. "Good." The osain flows through his hair and across his closed eyes. He is lifted up and sent into a nearby bathroom. Again he kneels; this time he is next to the bathtub. Again he closes his eyes, and again the osain is poured over his head; his godfather washes the back of his neck with soap and sings to the seat of his being, his head. The man is told to wash himself from head to toe with the osain and is left alone.

When he returns to the room, a cluster of objects stands in the middle of the floor. A cement head with cowrie shells for eyes, nose, and mouth sits in a small terracotta saucer, and next to it sits a smaller image that resembles it; these are Elegguá, the trickster, the lord of the crossroads and the ruler of destiny. Behind these stand a small, black iron cauldron; here is Ogún, the fierce and independent oricha of iron and warfare. With Ogún lives his brother Ochosi, the archer and god of the hunt; his power resides in the metal bow and arrow inside the cauldron. Next to the cauldron stands a metal cup that is closed and topped with a small rooster. This is Osun, a guardian who represents the neophyte's head; in it are the herbs used to make the osain. Osain pools in the saucers and in the cauldron, and drips down the metal shaft that elevates Osun. These orichas, the Guerreros, are the beginning of a person's "road in the saint." The man has come to "receive" them.[2]

Boxes are brought in from the patio. The godfather reaches into a box and pulls out a black rooster. He washes its underwings, the bottom of its feet, and its beak with clear water. He holds it by the legs, and its wings flap. The aleyo is told to turn slowly in a circle; as he rotates, he is brushed with the rooster in long sweeping motions from his head toward his feet. This is repeated until he has rotated completely. His hands are turned palm up and brushed with the bird's wings, then turned over and brushed again, and finally turned palm up and brushed a third time. The bird is stretched out and its neck cut. The blood flows onto Elegguá. Its head is placed next to Elegguá and its neck touches his saucers; the bird kicks, and the padrino pushes down hard to squeeze the air from the bird's lungs in order to quiet the animal. It kicks again and squeals; this time, the aleyo reaches down and forces the air from the bird and silences it. The slaughtering process is repeated with three doves, one each for Ogún, Ochosi, and Osun, and then again with a Guinea hen.

Following the *matanza* (Sp. slaughter), the aleyo is told to "do *moforibale*" (Lu. prostration). A mat is spread out in front of the orichas; his godfather stands next to them. The man lies down on the mat, first on his left side and then on his right. His knees are bent and his arm curls beneath his head as he "goes to the ground." "*¿Bueno?*" he asks. "Is this all right?" "Yes." He does moforibale to show his respect to the orichas that he has just received and to the oricha that "lives" in his godfather's head. His godfather touches his shoulders with his fingers and helps him up. The aleyo crosses his arms across his chest and is drawn to his elder's cheek, first on one side and then on the other. His padrino says softly, "*Santo. Ocha. Alafia*" (Lu. and Sp. saint, oricha, and peace, respectively). This gesture is repeated as he greets all of his elders and receives their blessings. George now belongs to their ritual family.

In an eastern city of the United States, this young man enters a new religious community; he is receiving a group of important deities and entering into ritual kin relationships with his initiators. He must have his head washed, his body cleaned by animals, and must perform the moforibale; to enter this tradition, he uses his body in ways that are new to him. As he receives the gods, he learns new patterns of body use. The creation of these new bodily patterns in the Guerreros initiation ritual presents an interesting case: the signs used in the ritual have meanings that can be communicated verbally, but here the signs are experientially apprehended through the body; they are not simply understood but also enacted. As he uses his body in new ways, his subjectivity is transformed.

In recent years, studies of cultural performances have demonstrated clearly that meaning is not latent in ritual signs and awaiting discovery; instead people involved in ritual performances engage signs and activate them (Schieffelin 1985:707). Through performance, people communicate cultural meanings; by employing the various culturally relevant and available communicative resources, including specific generic and gestural forms, people produce their culture. This production takes place in all cultured behavior, and ritual—any ritual—effectively opens the door to understanding the entire culture (V. Turner 1967).[3] Cultural performances "are occasions in which as a culture or society we reflect upon and define ourselves, dramatize our collective myths and history . . ." (MacAloon 1984a:1). Although communicative resources such as ritual do carry specific expectations for all involved, only through enactment and negotiation can meaning be established and understood. As Richard Bauman (1986:3) has written, "Performance, like all human activity, is situated, its form, meaning, and functions rooted in culturally defined scenes or events—bounded segments of the flow of behavior and experience that constitute meaningful contexts for action, interpretation, and evaluation." Cultural performances—performances of cultural forms— can have meaning and functions only when enacted (Abrahams 1977:95), and enactments often produce heightened experiences for participants.

Because this initiate, George, was not born into Santería, these experiences are new to him. These new bodily activities, quite common to the tradition, represent a change for George. To enter the tradition fully he must learn to use his body in new ways; he must master certain gestures and series of actions. As he experiences himself enacting new gestures and cultural forms of behavior, he realizes that his body is both a sign communicating meanings in a new way and simultaneously a locus of new experiences (Cowan 1990:4; cf. B. Turner 1984:1). His body is not simply a constructed sign that links him to the group (Douglas 1978:87); instead, the individual's body mediates all of the ritual signs, for he can only act by employing his body (cf. Ekman 1977). The enacting of these forms by the body represents the "modes of construction" of a culturally specific and useful body (Feher 1989:11). George needs to be able to enact each of the three gestures that I will explore in order to enter the religion more fully. He must understand *and* experience the importance of his head, he must learn the detailed gestures of sacrifice, and he must enact respect by prostrating himself in front of his elders. George learns to be a part of the community by using his body in specific ways.

This initiation ritual begins the establishment of new "habitual body sets, patterns of practical activity, and forms of consciousness" (Jackson 1989: 119–120). The activities of the ritual and the meanings therein are inseparable. In social action, an essential communicative form in Santería, pragmatic and semantic dimensions fuse; ideology is not an explicit discourse but an embodied, lived experience (Comaroff 1985:5). Because meaning merges with actions, the ritual represents the creation of a new *habitus* in the initiate; it is an enactment of some of the "principles of the generation and structuring of practices and representations" (Bourdieu 1989:72). Practitioners rarely provide detailed evaluations of social actions or of ceremonies, but they do refer to certain rituals as *bien hecha* (Sp. well done) or *linda* (Sp. beautiful). This choice of language suggests that the sought-after quality is aesthetic and nonanalytical—a kind of satisfaction or well-being. The manipulation of physical objects, those used on altars and in sacrifices as well as bodies, produces the elusive but desirable beautiful ceremony.[4]

This habitus represents a new social position for the neophyte in the case described earlier. This ritual is an important initiation on the road to the priesthood; it creates new bodily patterns for the initiate and thus inscribes the body into the new discourse. Previously abstract, verbal knowledge is enacted and incorporated. Never before has he had his head washed in osain; never before has he been cleaned by the sweepings of birds' wings; nor has he performed the moforibale. The giving and receiving of the Guerreros, repeated many times and in many places each year, assimilates people more fully into the community and gives them limited access to the supernatural world, and this example is no different. Here, however, the medium for assimilation is George. He must enact respect and embody the tradition.

This embodiment of tradition in the ritual context structures George's experience. As he uses his body in new ways and places it in new positions, he makes physical certain relationships and experiences them bodily; the initiation, then, regulates experience "through its capacity to reorganize the actor's experience of the situation" (Munn 1973:605). Although initiations vary according to the performers involved and these variations affect the structure of the ritual (Hanks 1984:131), the aleyo's body always structures the experience.

In Santería, the teaching of ritual skills and moral behavior happens informally and nonverbally, and thus embodiment is especially important. Ritual elders tire quickly of answering questions and suggest that the best method of learning is involvement. By paying attention and attending many rituals, an aleyo becomes known as *"serio"* (Sp. a serious [student of the religion]; see Friedman 1982). People do learn this religion through the exegesis of important concepts, but they learn primarily through observation and enactment. Because learning centers on practice and entering actively into this tradition, the body naturally emerges as central to any analysis of this kind of ritual (cf. Wafer 1991 on the body). This learning takes place slowly, so it is extremely difficult to document. The body exists in a complex relationship with social knowledge and interpretation. The informal learning style of Santería makes social knowledge a kind of esoteric power. People who know certain ceremonies exercise power in the community. My analysis reflects the social realities of this community. Ritual focuses on the body and its manipulation, and personal experience represents the primary method for understanding; when a practitioner integrates experience with more commonly held, culturally produced expressive forms such as divination stories, social knowledge is expanded. "The essential part of the *modus operandi* which defines practical mastery is transmitted in practice . . . without attaining the level of discourse" (Bourdieu 1989:87). The aleyo here clearly grasps this emphasis on practice and the use of the body; as George Carter remarks, "Although I had never done too much in Santería before, I, I guess I wanted to be part of the community which I was joining, to act like they do. I wanted to be involved and do what they did so I could learn the religion" (1990). Involvement must be physical to be complete; although George knows a great deal about the beliefs and sacred stories of Santería, he greatly values entering the habitus of the community and expects to learn from his experience.

It is important to note that neophytes who undergo rituals are not some-how miraculously transformed by some inexplicable and awesome power. Rather, ritualizations in Santería frequently place the individual in a series of ceremonies that engage many aspects of the individual's subjectivity. Virtually all initiations—including receiving the Warriors—result from divination rituals; as the previous chapter explains, these ceremonies evoke the specific aspects of the multiplex subjectivity of the client and then recontextualize them within the religious system. Divination almost always results in the prescription of additional ceremonies to address specific needs in the client's life; these rituals often overwhelm the human subject with repeated gestures, unfamiliar smells, alien sights, and unusual songs and other sounds. The sensory force of the ritual augments the emotional investment in the ceremony that results from the divination. After the ceremonies are completed, practitioners routinely socialize their experiences of transformation through narratives that focus on particular but patterned aspects of the process and on the role of the spirits and orichas in their lives. These narratives represent an important but uninvestigated area of mythological information within the religion, an area that is constantly renewing itself through social action and lived experience.

WASHING THE HEAD

Because no expressive bodily activity happens without real bodies and no meanings can be assigned to gestures without reference to a specific event (Poole 1975:101), the specific example at hand best reveals George's bodily practice. The community of ritual specialists washes George's head as he prepares to enter the community. He leans over with eyes closed to receive their attention and blessings. The herbal mixture "cools" his head and "refreshes" him. His head is washed over the basin and then again in the bathtub. Each time the priest rubs the osain and the herbs floating in it into his skin and scalp.

In the bathroom cleansing, which I have witnessed many times, the gestures of the ritual are highly stylized. The aleyo leans over the tub and places the chest on the edge; the hands rest on the bottom, one on top of the other. I have seen this priest, whom I will call José, demonstrate to people how they should position themselves as they receive the *despojo* (Sp. cleaning). Through this instruction in how properly to perform the gesture, José shows that he has an aesthetic by which he evaluates it. Similarly, José washes the head with a specific pattern of movements. He takes the osain from its basin in a small gourd and pours it first over the crown of the head and then over the neck. Again starting at the crown, he lathers the soap by moving it around the head in growing circles until he reaches the neck, which he scrubs vigorously. He then rinses the head with more osain and squeezes the water from the hair with a motion similar to the one with which he lathers it. These highly stylized gestures reveal a culturally structured pattern of bodily movement, and, although they are performed by the padrino, they suggest that the despojo does contain gestures that the aleyo learns and experiences through his body.

The head, which receives most of the attention in the cleaning, carries complex and multiple symbolic meanings in Santería. First, the head, called either orí or eledá, is the spiritual faculty and central locus of a human being (Murphy 1981:287). Before birth, each orí goes before the Creator and receives its essential character. This character, which people closely associate with an individual's destiny, can be either "hot" or "cool" (Cabrera 1980:121). Although practitioners disagree about how mutable the head's character is, the ritual washing here in refreshing herbs and water helps to cool a hot head. The head also idiomatically refers to the oricha that rules a person; an individual and the deity also establish this relationship in front of the Creator before birth (see Bascom 1991:115).

This central deity, often called "the owner of the head," represents an important part of the individual's character. For example, the white, calm, and generous oricha Obatalá rules the head of George's padrino, and so people assume that José is slow to anger, relatively intellectual, benevolent, and, others might add, "big-headed." In fact, at times practitioners confuse the "owner of the head" and the individual; "an Obatalá" refers to a child of Obatalá who in ritual may act in the role of that oricha. The eledá can be identified through various divination systems, and a growing relationship between an individual and the eledá often leads to initiations, after which the aché of the oricha literally resides inside the initiate's head; after a full initiation, the oricha can "mount" the initiate in trance possession and thus take control of the body that they share.[5]

In the Guerreros initiation, the aleyo, with the help of the oloricha, cleans and refreshes his head. Thus, the ritual attention to the head marks it as socially and religiously important. The osain is both an empowering and a cleaning agent; when applied to the head, it strengthens the spirit that dwells there. By cleaning the head, the ritual cools and refreshes the whole person. As the night goes on, after the aleyo departs from the site of the initiation, the leaves of the mixture, entwined in his hair, often begin to scratch and cause itching. George Carter recalls, "I felt a little strange scratching my head after José [his godfather] had spent so much time attending to it. He prayed and I scratched; it, it seemed so, so strange to treat what had been made sacred as something annoying, but my scalp really itched. Later, I said a prayer to my head [ruling oricha] in thanksgiving and slept with a white cloth over it"[6] (1990). This attention to the head, moreover, represents the beginning of a new cultural pattern. Many of the religion's rituals and customs underscore the centrality of the head. People entering Santería often start their affiliation when they need healing, and frequently the first ritual they undergo is the *rogación de la cabeza* (Sp. prayers for the head), where coconut, water, and cotton are applied to the head to "feed" it. Similarly, most practitioners cover their heads with hats (Sp. *gorros*) or handkerchiefs (Sp. *pañuelos*) during ritual activities. If their destinies include initiation, and they often do (Rogers 1973:28–29), their heads will receive still more attention.

Through various initiatory rites, the head is a focal point. Santería must be understood as an initiatory religion; initiations punctuate the changes and elevation of a person in the tradition. In one of the first initiations that a person receives, a priestess places necklaces (Lu. *eleke*, Sp. *collares*), consecrated, like the Guerreros, with herbal waters and the blood of sacrificial animals, over the neophyte's head and onto the shoulders. Each necklace has a different pattern of colored beads and conveys the power of one of the deities. An initiate most often receives the necklaces of the five most powerful and popular orichas; the necklaces, spiritually powerful and ritually charged, reflect the aché of each of them. The necklaces are both manifestations of the particular power of each deity and a channel for communication between the neophyte and the deities (Brandon 1983:355–356). They rest on the shoulders and reinforce the spiritual agent living in the head. Their form reflects the belief that the deities reside in the head. When the necklaces are received, the aleyo must again bow over a bathtub and have the head washed by the oloricha; all initiations include this bodily action of submission and reception of blessings.

The initiation of a full priest, capable of being mounted by an oricha, reiterates the attention on the head, that centralized idiom of spiritual power and life. In this ritual, the initiators wash the head of the neophyte and then shave it completely. The elders then mark the neophyte again, cutting a small cross into the top of the head; into this incision the initiators rub the most sacred herbs that contain the aché of the principal oricha. The head is covered with cloth, which will be worn for many hours to come. Finally the primary initiator crowns the neophyte with the tureens that contain the sacred stones that are the "spirit of the orichas" (Brandon 1983:397–401; see Ecún 1985 for examples of the variations within different initiations); the head, again, is the focus of the ritual.

During the ritual of receiving the Warriors, George receives Osun, an equivalent of his head. As I mentioned earlier, Osun contains the same herbs that are used to make the osain. When he receives Osun, he learns a simple ritual to call upon the oricha; thus he now has a simple but effective method of communication with a central part of himself.[7] If the aleyo continues in the religion and undergoes the full initiation, if he "makes the saint" (Sp. *hacer santo*), the practitioners will place an herbal mixture, called *aché de santo* (Lu. power of the saint), in the head and also place it within the Osun, which has a cup to receive this mixture. Thus, the Guerreros initiation, too, emphasizes the head beyond the cleansings. After this ritual the neophyte has an image of his head with which he can communicate. If the Osun falls, for example, the aleyo knows that danger is at hand.

The head, then, represents the bodily center of the spiritual life in Santería. Its import reveals itself throughout a variety of initiation ceremonies. Moreover, because other initiations repeat the cultural forms of this ritual, the Guerreros initiation anticipates a whole social and religious commitment to the Santería comunity. The head receives respect because "the head carries the body."[8] As the seat of spiritual power and possibility, as the place that the ruling oricha dwells, people associate the head with destiny or "the road of life." Elder priests and priestesses clean the head, feed it, and sing to it. While George experiences these things he is literally incorporating important values in Santería. Although he may reflect upon them as the actions happen through his physical involvement and the attention to his head, he joins a wider practice that is common to all people involved in Santería. Similarly, it anticipates other cleanings, sacrifices, and initiations that are socially constituted and bodily enacted and learned.

The social actions that focus on the head do not reveal the meanings of the initiation. The meanings, communicated through signs, do not lie in a separate plane outside the immediate domain of actions (Jackson 1989:122). The actions of these people as they enact the ritual bespeak a commonality.

It is because actions speak louder *and* more ambiguously than words that they are more likely to lead us to common truths; not semantic truths, established by others at other times, but experiential truths which seem to issue from within our own Being [*sic*] when we break the momentum of the discursive mind or throw ourselves into some collective activity in which we each find our own meaning yet at the same time sustain the impression of having a common cause and giving common consent. (Jackson 1989:133)

This passage argues the extreme importance and power of signs and their messages for the *participants* of ritual; participants, by both framing events personally and conforming to the larger social and cosmological order that the ritual communicates, come to embody the very contrast of structure and agency. By enacting the ritual, the initiate accepts socially and publicly the order that the ritual signifies (Rappaport 1989:469). George and his padrinos act together and, regardless of any other conflicts that they have, they serve his head and thus care for his essence. George expresses that attention as he leans over the basins to make his head available, and his padrinos show it in gestures of washing. Here, through these actions, as George accepts this cultural emphasis on the head, he begins to accept the new habitus of the religion.

"MAKING SACRIFICE"

By receiving the Guerreros, George Carter "opens the roads" for himself by "making sacrifice" (Lu. *rubó,* Sp. *hacer ebó*). He is committing himself not simply to the members of ritual house, nor is he simply attending to his head; he is also committing himself to a life-long relationship with the Warriors themselves, and this relationship will include, at a minimum, a regular weekly offering to the orichas. However, it is likely that he will have to sacrifice other animals in the future. The initiation is the first time that George has witnessed the sacrifice of birds, and he now is religiously bound to make regular sacrifices himself. Thus, sacrifice represents another form of behavior in which George participates at his initiation but that he must also learn to enact himself.

In the sacrifice, the birds are washed. Holding them by the feet, José brushes each animal across the aleyo to sweep off any negative influences that may be lingering on George. Slowly José sweeps from the head down toward the feet. An oloricha draws back the birds' wings and holds their feet; with the Guinea hen and the rooster, José pulls the neck to extend it, then pierces it with a knife, and the blood runs down the knife and onto the awaiting orichas. The doves receive similar treatment; however, instead of cutting their necks, José bends their necks to the side and then plucks them off. Because a special initiation confers the right to use a sacrificial knife, the aleyo will have to pull the heads off any birds he sacrifices to feed his Warriors. These formal processes, which George is witnessing and learning, will represent an essential aspect of his religious life in the future.

Whenever divination suggests the need, George will feed his Warriors. He will gather the necessary birds and perform this ceremony, which is central to the religion. Just as he has witnessed at his initiation, he will wash the birds' underwings, their heads, and their feet. He will say the prayers and sing the *cantos* (Sp. chants) that he has heard and learned. Although he may not understand the Lucumí words that he uses, he will stretch out the birds and pull their heads off to slaughter them. He will mimic the way he has seen matanzas performed and thus will constitute his own tradition within the tradition. Because he has never before witnessed sacrifice, the initiation represents a crucial moment of learning for George. He watches, and he learns new behaviors. As he said of the experience, "I was anxious because I had never seen a matanza before, but I guess, well, I was also, I think I wanted to see how to do it so I could feed my Eleggua and give him the blood and do works. I had read the songs and the prayers in different places, and I had read about sacrifices, but I knew that seeing one would teach me even more. Only if I saw a sacrifice would I know how to do one" (1990). By watching, George learns what he cannot learn elsewhere; he understands what gestures to perform in a sacrifice.

Perhaps the most striking example of this learning lies not in the future sacrifices that George will make but in the event itself. When the rooster continues to move and make noise after its head is severed, José leans on it to force the air from its lungs. When the bird again kicks and squeals, George, imitating what he has just seen, quiets the bird. "I wanted to try and see how to do it. I wanted to quiet that bird *with my own two hands*" (Carter 1990). This moment represents the essence of the initiation process. Here George is observing the "techniques of the body" that Santería employs (Mauss 1973), but he goes beyond simple observation and uses his body in ways that are new to him: he enacts culturally specific behavior and practices his performance.

By forcing the air from the rooster, he shows the community around him not only that he wants to be a member but also that he will act in appropriate ways. He begins to assert his competence (Bauman 1977:11), although, as a person with the status of a child, he risks failing. But he has successfully acquired an understanding of how this gesture is used (see Hymes 1974:75) and thus begins to act socially within this religious community. Because social action has a kind of power in the community, George asserts himself as a serio. By mimicking his padrino, George performs a relatively unimportant ritual task; the ritual in no way revolves around quieting the rooster, but is a bit more pleasant for everyone because of it. Quieting the bird also demonstrates that George is willing and capable of entering the tradition. Here he performs his membership in the group; the tradition diffuses as people enact specific gestures, and the aleyo follows the lead of his godfather[9]: "Carter is a serious guy and he is not afraid to jump into things. If I do something in a ritual, he repeats. . . . He will be a good santero when the time comes. He will be a good santero because he puts himself into a ceremony and doesn't hesitate" (González 1992).

Just as the sacrifice itself is an important practice that George learns in the initiation, the sweeping of the body by animals for cleansing purposes represents another traditional behavior that he begins to enact. Rubbing rituals use animals or fruit to remove negative influences, and they represent an entire subclass of ritual offerings to the deities. Diviners frequently suggest these "works" (Lu. *ebó*, Sp. *trabajos*). Here George is learning the correct speed to turn and the gestures that are done with the hands. As he goes through these acts, he again learns culturally specific behavior. As he turns and is swept by the wings, George is again acquiring the practical and bodily patterns of Santería ritual.

MOFORIBALE: I BOW MY HEAD TO THE GROUND

Although previous work on cultural performances has focused on the role of individuals as signs (see Stoeltje 1988) and the presentation of social structure for reflection (for example, see Stoeltje and Bauman 1989), authors have not embraced an ongoing examination of the process of learning a social and cosmological order through performance. Performance studies must account for the production and maintenance of social relationships by actors in the social field (McArthur 1989:115); "ritual action effects social transitions or spiritual transformations; it does not merely mark or accompany them" (MacAloon 1984b:250). The ritual causes change simply by its occurrence; it expresses and communicates its meanings with or without the participants' consent or knowledge (Myerhoff 1984:170).

The moforibale represents an important religious behavior that George

acquires during his initiation and through which he performs his social obligations.[10] After the washing and after the divinities eat, he must "put his
head to the ground" in front of his padrino and the other members of his
ritual family. Because the oricha that "owns his head" is female, he must
go down on each side with his head facing the direction of the oricha he is
honoring. If the aleyo's head were male, the moforibale would have a different form; instead of reclining on each side, a person ruled by a male
oricha must prostrate with the forehead on the floor and the arms and legs
extended straight out. Here the body gesture marks the gender of the ruling oricha and not the person; the gender of the oricha defines the way the
person must bow. Again, as in the previous discussion of the despojo, the
stylization of these gestures reiterates their cultural significance. José explains how to go down, and then George lies down; he asks if he is doing
it correctly. His padrino raises him and blesses him. This series of gestures
is central to the kinship that the ritual creates.

I had seen people do the moforibale before, and I knew that it was an important
form of respect. Respect is important in Santería. We have to respect the elders
because we receive the orichas from their hands. The dead gave birth to the orichas. That's a proverb that means we have to show respect. . . . My head doesn't
have a saint in it so I have to put it on the floor in front of my padrino, whose head
does have an oricha in it. (Carter 1990)

Here George articulates the complexity of the moforibale, which indexes a
series of important relationships. One head honors another by going to the
floor. A new initiate shows respect to a ritual elder. By going to the floor,
George enacts spatial, social, and cosmic relationships.

By receiving the Guerreros, the aleyo becomes attached to the initiator's
ritual family and begins a serious commitment to the religious community.
By receiving the Warriors, neophytes commit themselves to a life-long relationship with not only the oloricha but also the ritual house, the wider
religious community that congregates at important festivals. Inside this
community exists a complex family of ritual kin (Brandon 1983:480; cf.
D. Brown 1989:162–186). The initiating priest, after the ritual, becomes
the padrino and the neophyte the *ahijado* or *ahijada* (Sp. godson, goddaughter). This relationship entails mutual commitment, and both parties
are expected to treat the other as a family member (Murphy 1988:83; cf.
D. Brown 1989:174–186). Just as parents raise a child, so too will the godparents enculturate the aleyo; they demonstrate the proper behavior, and

the aleyo learns by following their example; they "speak without a voice" (Flores 1990:49).

Ritual kinship is construed in terms of *casas* or *ilé* (Sp., Lu. houses) and *ramas* (Sp. branches, lineages). A house is a single oloricha and the people initiated by that person. Filial relationships occur at every initiation, and thus a person can have many ahijados and many padrinos simultaneously. Those previously initiated by José become George's brothers and sisters "in the saint." To differentiate between different kinds of godchildren, José refers to individuals by the initiations that they have received from him; for example, after this initiation George becomes his ahijado de Guerreros (Sp. godson of the Warriors). These lines of relationship are traced through generations of living and dead ritual forebears. Thus, José's godmother *de asiento* (Sp. of the full initiation) becomes George's grandmother in the saint (Sp. *abuela de santo*).[11] These larger groups are the ramas that connect people across time. Just as an aleyo descends from a godparent and ritual ancestors, the orichas are also "born" from each other. George's Warriors are born from José's. Ritual elders (Sp. *mayores*) expect respect, and moforibale expresses that honor concretely and directly (D. Brown 1989:170).

The moforibale reiterates social order as it exists and as sanctioned by the morality of Santería tradition. For example, an aleyo, when needing help from the orichas, employs a godparent as intermediary or, at the very least, as a guide. This relationship subordinates the uninitiated to those with experience within the religion. The godparents have knowledge, spiritual power, and, according to Santería morality, a social responsibility. In the Guerreros initiation, George must approach the orichas with the aid of his ritual family.

By working the orichas—that is, being initiated, attending as many rituals as possible, and serving the community—the aleyo gains knowledge; however, that knowledge remains, by definition, social (Gregory 1986: 141). Increased skill with the orichas increases his responsibility both to the orichas and to his ritual house. Initiation creates access to ritual knowledge; it attaches the neophyte to the house's members, both living and dead. Although the hierarchical system of initiations limits and regulates the access to ritual skill, people learn the skills themselves in social interaction within the ritual house. Degree and seniority of initiation determine the ritual status and social responsibility of a practitioner; to act within these boundaries is to act "coolly."

In the moforibale, the touching of the head to the floor, a ritually younger person salutes the "head" of the elder. Thus, George honors José's oricha; he physically submits his oricha to the oricha of his elder.

By enacting this social and religious hierarchy, George publicly shows his acceptance of his new relationship with José and the submission that it implies. This public display makes the body a focus of interaction, and so it becomes an important locus of self-definition in the social context (see Glassner 1990:222; Mead 1938:292). Although he will "have" the Warriors after this initiation, he still needs his godparents to help him solve problems and teach him how to interact with the orichas. The moforibale is a bodily performance of this relationship.[12]

After "going down," George is raised by his padrino and blessed. The reciprocal relationship is complete. George honors José's head and receives a blessing: "The raising is a blessing which elevates, strengthens, and honors the junior . . . a sign of ritual recognition: symbolically conveying, affirming and supporting membership in a relationship" (Yvette Burgess-Polcyn, quoted in D. Brown 1989:171). The body physically learns and enacts this ritual greeting and display of honor. The body and its position communicate the respect, and the raising changes the relationship. But this relationship is not just projected onto the body; the body's gesture constructs and communicates it. George conceives of the moforibale as an important act: "I was glad and excited to [mo]foribale in front of José and my Guerreros. It felt strange to be, to be on the floor in the middle of a room with people all around, but . . . I just felt that I had to do it to show my respect and fit into the ilé. It seemed even weirder to go down for the other olorichas that I didn't even know" (Carter 1990). George must perform the moforibale repeatedly to show his respect for all who are his elders in the saint; despite its distinct and foreign feel, he goes down because he wants to show his respect to the people who have brought him into the religion.[13] What is perhaps more important, he goes down to act as other people in the ilé act, "to fit in." By reproducing an important cultural form in a noticeable social space, he embodies a social position and continues to maintain the status relationships.

EMBODIED MEANINGS AND LIVING TRADITIONS

This initiation is, indeed, a rite of passage. But an approach that relies on such a structural analysis, which isolates form and social function from more personal meaning, ignores an entire aspect of the ritual. Rather than focus on the patterns in the ritual structure, highlighting the forms the aleyo must enact alters the emphasis of interpretation. If we are to understand how transformations of subjectivity and social status are accomplished and experienced, the initiate's body must remain central to the analysis. The experience of transformation in rites of passage surely includes something more complicated and more delicate than the tripartite structure as put forth (see Van Gennep 1909; V. Turner 1969:94–130). People and their experiences always overflow the concepts and categories that social scientists use to comprehend them. I am advocating a more individual approach to this kind of material. How does the initiate use the body before and after the ritual? What effect does the change have on other aspects of life? Is the new habitus limited to one context, or does it spill into other parts of the person's life? (For excellent examples of body-focused analyses of rites of passage, see V. Turner 1967, 1969:1–93.)

The meaning of this initiation cannot be understood without reference to the bodily practices of the initiate. It is by using his body in new ways and performing specific gestures that George enters into the religion. Through performing these specific cultural forms, through attending to his head in various ways, through sacrificing and all its gestures, through going to the floor in the moforibale, he enacts his membership in his new religious context and venerates the gods. Under the guidance of his initiators, he transforms his subjectivity. The bodily reproduction of socially prescribed behaviors keys the emergent meanings of the initiation; through enactment practitioners display their relationships with each other and the forces of the universe. Moreover, the meaning of the signs in these rituals lies not so much in their abstract meanings but in how they are experienced through the body of the aleyo. The meanings of the signs are only accessible and sensible through the use of the body. As Pierre Bourdieu observes, "Rites, more than any other type of practice, serve to underline the mistake of enclosing them in concepts a logic made to dispense with concepts; of treating movements of the *body* and practical manipulations as purely logical operations" (1989:116, italics mine).

People learn the bodily and social practice of Santería through initiation; by experiencing a new habitus, the aleyo joins his new tradition. Although he has understood the tradition in an intellectual way and has studied a great deal, by joining a ritual family and offering a sacrifice, he places himself into the practical life of the religion. He knows the tradition in a different way now, and he feels different as well. Now he understands the worship of the orichas and some of their stories, and he also knows how to worship them. In Santería, personal identity, social relationships, and ritual knowledge are performed by people as they bow their heads to the ground.

3

"MY PANTS ARE BLOODY"

Negotiating Identity in American Santería

Late on a cold December evening in 1990, an oríaté and I quickly climb into a small car. We have just finished an initiation ritual in which I became an ahijado by receiving a group of divinities called the Guerreros and in which seven birds were sacrificed.[1] The blood seemed to go everywhere—on sacred objects, on the floor, and on the walls. We rush to Union Station in Washington, D.C., where we are going to retrieve a friend of the oríaté who has come from New Jersey for another godchild's "birthday in the saint" (Sp. *cumpleaños de santo*); we are hurrying because the visitor has already been waiting for a couple of hours. The car pulls into the circle in front of the grand station, hung with huge wreaths for Christmas, and slows to a stop. As the oríaté climbs from the car, he looks down at his white pants and stops in his tracks. *"Mis pantalones están sangrientos,"* he says. "My pants are bloody." He looks anxious. He is visibly shaken. I laugh, astonished by his concern, saying *"¡Así es la vida de un oríaté!"* (Such is the life of an oríaté!) Together we enter the deserted train station. A single Afro-Cuban man sits on a bench off to one side. His hair is in a mohawk, and he is stylishly dressed. It is for him that we have come.

The diviner is concerned about his appearance, about his self-presentation in this location. Although blood seems appropriate in the house where the initiation takes place, here, in this more public context, the same man is upset by its presence. He is aware that blood will draw attention to him and that people will imagine that he is a violent man. That the same person can have opposite reactions to the same thing in the matter of an hour raises the question: Why is the blood acceptable at the house and not acceptable at the train station? This change in attitude reflects something larger about the diviner's life; he has diverse interests and must work to manage himself in such a way that those interests, which are always present and often contradictory and are simultaneously the very basis of his life, are reconciled. Although he may be performing (Goffman 1959:17), that metaphor for social life distorts the most common experiences of people as they live; I am sure that José, the same oríaté I discussed in the previous chapter, would not agree that he was acting or performing.

Building on the previous discussions of personal identity and the embodiment of certain key values in the religion, this chapter asks related questions: How do people in the religion negotiate their many social roles and relationships? How do different roles in their lives imply different interests and commitments? What model of the person—the human subject—can allow and account for such changes? I address these questions by examining this moment and a few similar ones that I observed during the same birthday festivities in 1990.

Rather than simply explore the social rules and constructions by which individual persons are constituted and defined in Santería culture, it is necessary to examine the particular circumstances and experiences of a real human subject. My project attempts something different from certain writers who have addressed the more general notions of person (for example, see Geertz 1973). Although the general social conventions about personhood inform this project, it focuses on a more subjective experience of those notions by individuals. This difference—between the "moral person" and the "me" of an individual's experience (see Mauss 1938)—represents a shift in anthropological work from an emphasis on the generically social to the exploration of more personalized meanings and experiences. Despite the presence in every culture of concepts of person and standards and models for ethical behavior in the negotiation of personal interests, a focus on an individual's lived experience is primary here. The idiosyncratic aspects come to the fore; different strategies for coping with conflicting interests become significant markers of individuality, and personal choices represent fundamental moments in which people assert particular "contingencies" that make them unique (Rorty 1989:25).

José, after noticing that blood has covered the floor and the wall at the place of the sacrifice, blood from an animal that he has killed, is surely aware that it may have splattered on his pants. Still, at the train station, his genuine surprise reflects his changed understanding of the situation: the station represents another frame and forces him to evaluate himself in a different light. José "sees" himself as outside the norms of this new location and situation; he knows that bloody pants are not appropriate for a public and national place like Union Station, which sits just a couple of blocks from the Capitol. As a Cuban American, intensely patriotic, he greatly values being accepted into American culture.[2] He fears revealing that he practices blood sacrifice in a social setting where such behavior is unacceptable; although he can manage his behavior as he interacts with people at the station, he cannot so easily control how those he meets will interpret his bloody pants. Regardless of the rest of his demeanor and self-expression, his commitment to sacrifice is at the very least indexed by the blood.

The complexity of the situation can be approached in several edifying ways. To begin, José is deeply conscious of his enduring commitment to Santería. This man left Cuba, at least in part, because he wanted to become more involved in the religion and, for various reasons, was unable to receive any initiations there (Velásquez 1990b). He "made the saint" in 1982; since that time he has initiated some forty other people into the religion and received many smaller initiations himself. He holds a job that allows him to travel often; he frequently visits New York on weekends to participate in religious activities there (Velásquez 1990b). Because many of his godchildren and his godparents live in New Jersey and New York City, José has chosen a lifestyle that allows him to make the four-hour trek regularly.

Similarly, José's house is a center for Santería ritual life in the Washington area. José divines for twenty or thirty people every week and works every day of the week as an oríaté (Velásquez 1990b). On almost any night, a visitor to his house will encounter other people waiting to consult with him; because of demands on his time, it is common for him, after returning home from a full-time day job around six in the evening, to work until one or two in the morning. During the day people call and speak to his wife María; because of her close association with José and the fact that she is also a priestess in the religion, she is able to assist many godchildren who need advice about ritual practice. In addition to passing along information, María regularly keeps track of José's many appointments.

This religious commitment does not lack self-interest. Without doubting José's devotion to the saints, it is important to understand that for each ritual activity that he performs, José receives a *derecho*. Though in theory a sacrifice to the oricha involved in the ritual, these fees do represent important income for José and his family. For example, for the initiation of receiving the Guerreros, the new godson paid a derecho of $750.[3] From this money, supplies (fruit, herbs, animals) were purchased and derechos paid to the other santeros who helped in the work. Thus, these ritual activities are both acts of devotion and income-producing opportunities.

Because José is so deeply devoted to his religious life, I am hesitant to interpret his concern about the blood on his pants as a rejection of that part of his life. His comment transcends this moment. Instead, I imagine him noticing a detail that is out of place in the new environment. The frame changes as he climbs from the car. What before seemed normal now represents an outstanding and outlandishly noticeable problem. Blood has a different meaning here than it did at the house or in the car. Whereas it now marks José as different from those around him, a difference potentially intensified in this public, Anglophone space by José's inability to speak English—before he left the car the blood signified indexically his involvement and commitment to Santería and other practitioners of the religion.

Not only does the train station create a new frame for understanding the blood, but it also represents a change in "front" (Goffman 1959:22). His front—his self-presentation, "which regularly functions in a general and fixed fashion to define the situation" (Goffman 1959:22)—so focused on a Santería "audience," must change to fit the new situation. Here, in a moment of intense reflexivity, José evaluates himself, and again the notion of a complex and multiplicitous subject emerges. As I said before, he "sees" himself and assesses what he sees.

Without straying into an overly complex and convoluted psychological analysis of the cognitive dissonance produced by this self-observation, I want to underscore that José here becomes a sign of himself to himself. The blood marks a different, more private aspect of José's life; in the public space of the station, this person seems inappropriate to José himself, and its presence disrupts his experience of himself. Here two semiotic and socially given categories of the person are at play in the same moment. This lived experience of the moral person can be referred to as the *self*. It is critical to understand that this self is not purely personal, but rather an individual's lived experience of the limiting and emergent qualities of the culture; there is no transcendent "inner experience," but rather an inner dialogue with socially given signs (Voloshinov 1973:39). Any description of the self is always done with words from a language and is therefore "a semiotic expression of the contact between the organism and the outside environment" (Voloshinov 1973:26). In this case, José wishes to eclipse one self with another that he anticipates will be more acceptable to the American "audience" at hand. As he changes roles he changes models of personhood, and therefore has different rights and responsibilities. Different actions and interests come into play depending on the situation in which José finds himself; his parallel selves emerge in succession (cf. Elster 1986:13–20)[4]; he shows a series of different identities and social affiliations in a short time.

But as José reveals his concern about the new situation to his godson and "performs" himself, he also reveals the fundamental diversity of his own experiences. In this example, he comments about his appearance. His concern, as already discussed, may relate to the new environment. Similarly, he may be concerned about his visitor's response to and evaluation of the bloody pants. The visitor, whom I will call Roberto, may judge José harshly because of the blood, even though Roberto is also a santero. Roberto habitually dresses in the latest fashion. The first time I met him in May 1990, he was dressed in shorts and two matching tank-top T-shirts worn together, creating an intense mix of neon pinks and greens that accented the colorful beads that santeros habitually wear for religious reasons. On this particular night in December, he wore black slacks, a black silk shirt, and black shoes with silver metal on the uppers. His hair is consistently in a wide, flat mohawk. He had a necklace of large, African trade beads—white with blue stripes—to honor the oricha of disease and healing, Babalú-Ayé; around his left wrist he wore a stunning and elaborate bracelet in similar colors, also for Babalú-Ayé. Roberto's seemingly "endless devotion to style," as he expressed it, perhaps intimidates José, who also tries to dress well. For clarity, let me state that fashion is neither my academic specialty nor my personal passion; still, these observations do add another important dimension to the discussion at hand. If cultural acts emerge from situational and social contexts, then José's concern about his bloody pants must be related to the social context in which he finds himself. As Richard Bauman writes, "The structure of . . . events is a product of the interplay of numerous situational factors, including physical setting, *participants' identities and roles,* cultural ground rules for performance, norms of interactions and interpretation, and the sequence of actions" (1983:365, italics mine). To some extent, then, the context shapes the participants' roles and identities, just as they are shaped by it.

As I have remarked, the pants distinguish between the hours at the house doing ritual work and the present public location. This moment of José's life, in the American world that is somewhat alien to him because of language and cultural barriers against Cuban Americans, contrasts sharply with the recent past, when he ate Cuban-style chicken with beans and rice with his extended ritual family, all of whom speak Spanish more easily than English. The issue of the past and present is especially important to Cuban Americans living in exile; the present in the United States often contrasts drastically with the past in Cuba. Many Cuban Americans suffer from a cultural malady called the *gorrión* (Sp. lit. sparrow, fig. "the blues"), whose common symptoms include a yearning for Cuba and a general nostalgia for all that has been left behind.

José's complex reaction to the blood on his pants shows, as I have argued, his commitments to a great many things: to his religious life and family, to his nation, to his relationship with Roberto. He reveals himself as a "multiple presence" of "infinite layers" (Trinh 1989:94): past, present, social life internalized and externalized. These differences, all contained within José's life, do not annul identity but aid in its creation (Trinh 1989:104); his experience of himself includes all these times and relationships, not to mention the feelings that he has about them, and it is precisely remembered moments, like the dinner with his family and his Cuban childhood, and specific relationships that make him most naturally and completely himself (Abrahams 1986b:56). I do not intend a "simplistic definition of identity" (Spivak 1990:38); instead I offer questions about the "experiencing subject" (Bruner 1986:9). An experiencing subject can be seen as a function of social relationships. Individuals are equated with their social roles. José is a *man*, an *oríaté*, a *lover*, a *son*, a *father*, a *husband*, and a *Cuban American*. Each of these social positions has a folk group attached to it with attendant relationships, roles, and commitments (Dundes 1980); he is none of these things in isolation. Yet, paradoxically, José is all these things at once. Similarly, he fits into many rhetorical positions; he is *yo* (Sp. I) when speaking and *tú* or *usted* (Sp. you) when addressed (Lacan 1978:298); he occupies no singular position in social life or discourse. Still, his identity and subjectivity can be seen "as an emergent property of historicized experience" (Alcoff 1988:431). Thus, José as an experiencing subject exists in a specific historical context that acts as a frame and helps create meaning (Alcoff 1988:434; Jackson 1989:13). He experiences himself and the events of his life through all these lenses.[5] As Michael Jackson writes, "The 'self' cannot, therefore, be treated as a thing among things; it is a function of our involvement with others in a world of diverse and ever-altering interests and situations" (1989:3). Social roles and groups frame what people experience and thus give it a specific kind of meaning (Goffman 1974), but this meaning is never final, exclusive, or determinate. Yet neither José nor his experience can be reduced to these facts of social life (Sartre 1969). He is more than the sum total of his social positions.

Still, each social role and each social situation carries with it expectations of certain kinds of behavior and different commitments (see Goffman 1959:13). These differences, interarticulated throughout a day, a month, a life, combine with the reactions of other people to reiterate José's self-objectification: "In declaring that the human being has a self," Herbert Blumer remarks, "[George Herbert] Mead had in mind that the human being can be the object of his own actions. He can act toward himself as others might act toward him" (1969:79). Thus, he can anticipate, through remembering past experiences and well-known social expectations, how people might judge him in different situations; he knows full well that Euro-Americans will react negatively to blood sacrifice. To this must be added his relationship to his new godson and to Roberto. Each of these interests comes to play a part in José's response to the blood. As Michel Maffesoli writes, "For the same social fact there can be a multiplicity of causes" (1985:58).

The following evening at the birthday party for the orichas, people socialize as they eat Cuban food and drink beer. As people enter throughout the evening, they greet the orichas before the *trono* (Sp. throne, an ornate altar) by having an elder pray for them or doing moforibale. In this way, they pay homage to the pure and kind oricha Obatalá on his "birthday." This is all very calm, very common. A Panamanian woman kneels before the trono to pray.[6] Unlike everyone else, she begins to quiver and shake. Suddenly the room falls silent. Everyone's attention focuses on the young woman's body. The woman who is giving the trono, Idaberta, makes "passes" behind the neck of the Panamanian woman, trying to coax the invading spirit to depart. A voice—not the voice of the woman—announces that the oricha wants toasted corn and incense to be added to the throne. Idaberta rushes into the next room and returns with the required offerings. The spirit throws the corn toward the back of the throne, a huge construction of cloth that contains the orichas. The spirit then lights the incense and inhales deeply. Suddenly, she slumps back and pulls her hand across her forehead. The woman has returned and is offered a place near the throne.

In Santería culture, "controlling" various aspects of individual agency is greatly valued.[7] Just as I have argued that there are multiple kinds of agency and the lived experience of different social commitments—multiple selves—at work in José's experience of his life, the "socially constructed ideology of personhood" is also multiple (Jacobson-Widding 1990:31): To begin, there are several souls of different classes. Every person is believed to have a deity that "rules" or "owns the head"; this oricha is often called *eledá,* but also alternately *orí* (both mean head). This part of a person's being is expected to exercise some influence over personality; for example, José is ruled by the white, calm, and generous oricha Obatalá, and from this information, a person can assume that he will be slow to anger, relatively intellectual, benevolent, and, others might add, "big-headed." In fact, at times the eledá and the individual are confused by people; a child of Obatalá may be referred to as "an Obatalá," and in ritual may act in the role of the oricha. The eledá is, according to myth, chosen before birth by each individual (see Bascom 1991:115), and can be identified through various divination systems. A growing relationship between an individual and the eledá often leads to initiations, in which the aché of the oricha is literally put inside the initiate's head; after initiation, the oricha can safely "mount" the initiate in trance possession.

As well as having a ruling deity, each individual also possesses a *cuadro espiritual* (Sp. lit. spiritual portrait) made up of various egun who protect and bless the person. It is not uncommon for a single person to have as many as twenty-five *protectores* (Sp. protective ancestral spirits) as the primary members of a cuadro. For example, María has two primary guides: a male American Indian and an Afro-Cuban woman who worked as a priestess of the oricha of the sea, Yemayá—just as María is now. These spirits are represented by a life-size cigar store Indian and a large doll seated on a wicker throne; these dynamic representations are used to interact with the spirits but are not considered to be the spirits themselves. The ritual ancestors of a person's religious house are also venerated. Just as the orichas can possess, so too can the egun.

Possession by both the orichas and the ancestors must be controlled. Despite the fact that contact with these beings is desirable and pursued in ritual, unrequested mountings usually evoke extraordinarily harsh judgments from those present. A person who "passes" (Sp. *pasar*) a spirit when not trying to is assumed to have offended the spirit in some way. Although this is an interesting phenomenon in its own right, I am interested here in the fact that possession, an important aspect to the religious system, must be negotiated just like every other commitment and every other manifestation of agency. The Panamanian woman knelt before the throne for Obatalá and passed an egun who proceeded to make demands on behalf of the orichas: The incense and toasted corn were offered to the gods, but the woman became the focus of conversation and action for quite a while. José and Roberto, as the senior priests present, paid careful attention to the spirit, but the woman was criticized almost immediately after coming out of trance. Because she had passed an egun at an inappropriate time and place, Roberto assumed that she was also suffering in other areas of her life and concluded that she must be ill. This example serves to demonstrate again the notion that selves with different interests, although all valued, are tied to different contexts and roles.

It is interesting to add that in my field notes I sketched out a rather condemning interpretation of this woman's behavior. Because she arrived with a young son who was repeatedly nagging her for attention during the entire evening and whom she repeatedly rebuffed, and because the people that I know the best in this community—José, María, and Idaberta—all disapproved of this "invading" spirit and its medium, I wrote a brief psychological interpretation that suggested that the woman, upset with the demands of motherhood in this context, passed the spirit to gain the attention that she wanted from other members of the community. What is of particular interest here is that I was willing in the moment and shortly thereafter to assume the role of judging this woman negatively, just as my closest companions in the community had. So much for any remnant of objectivity in fieldwork. This example underscores the importance of radical empiricism's mixture of the subjective and the objective perspectives in the ethnographic enterprise.

What I documented were the evaluations of my closest companions in this house. Acceding to their negative reaction to this behavior, I fashioned an interpretation focused on this woman's conscious and unconscious intentions in this context. I listened to the voices of my "informants," but what they said were not "cultural truths"; instead they provided me with their responses to this woman and her spirit's behavior in this circumstance, a moment that included many outsiders unfamiliar with the violent onset of possession as well as this inquisitive *gringo* (Sp. outsider) who asked a lot of questions and took notes (see Hastrup 1992:121). The result was a fixing of a moment in a social process and the beginning of an interpretation of that moment by a particular, historically situated subject.

All ethnographers are positioned subjects and cope with and understand certain phenomena better than others (R. Rosaldo 1984:192). My position is defined by age, gender, and my status as a relative outsider, but my experiences previous to this fieldwork moment enabled me to see certain things while it eclipsed others. If participation as method is taken seriously and if the intersubjective aspects of fieldwork are exploited, then the fieldworker is repositioned in the field. Her "self" is blurred by the change of social context, by relational and inventive nature of identities both within the field and in the academy (Clifford 1988:10), and by never-ending educational dialogue that creates the notes that lead to this text (see Hastrup 1992:117–120). This disruption in the ethnographer's self leads to all sorts of anxiety, and "methodology may often be a locus of displacement for the anxiety provoked not just by the data but by the investigator's confrontation with the subjects of the research" (Crapanzano 1977:69). In this case, my confrontation with this unpredictable spirit and my involvement with certain members of the house led to a specific understanding of the events, despite the fact that I had recently received the Warriors within this same house.

Upon reflection, I adumbrated an interpretation of the events I had witnessed and whose implications I had heard from my friends. My colleagues had given me an "insider's" conception of the incident, and I took their words and transformed them into a still simpler interpretation. José, Roberto, and Idaberta all gave me accounts of what had happened and the difficulties in the woman's character that led to the event. And because understanding is always tied to language, I used their language as the starting place for my own account of their acquaintance's behavior, but not without translating their ideas into a frame of reference more in keeping with the genre of field notes and more closely akin to the disciplines of folklore, anthropology, and the study of religion.

Interpretation of another culture always includes the translation of one set of ideas and events from one cultural frame of reference to another (Giddens 1993:170). This double hermeneutic always requires first the use of the "local" system of knowledge and then the use of the discourse of the human sciences. The metalanguage that I chose in this small case echoes the metalanguage of subjectivity, personhood, and self that I am using throughout this volume. I sketch out this process to draw attention to the provisional quality of all interpretation and to the fact that this work results from a long process of social interaction between my interlocutors and me. This moment of reflexivity underscores a third hermeneutical moment that reconsiders social interactions and results—however schematically—in the production of knowledge (Karp and Kendall 1982:271; see also Babcock 1980:11 and Karp 1986:134–135). My selves, too, are implicated in the production of this ethnography and in the social life I describe.

But how are the interests of these different selves negotiated in the course of daily life? In Santería, an individual is constantly trying to maintain a balance between the spiritual and the material worlds. Upon this search for balance the ritual system is constructed. Divination, a central aspect of ritual practice, provides a method for the spirits, both orichas and egunes, to address human beings. Sacrifice, another key element in the system, allows humans to communicate with the spirits. In possession the human and the spirit are united briefly in the same body (see Murphy 1981 for a fuller account of this schema). A balance leads to the maximum accumulation of aché, the essential power to accomplish things. Thus, balance with the spiritual leads to prosperity, health, and other physical blessings. Perhaps the most common method to discern paths to balance is divination; the divination stories (Sp. *historias;* Lu. *pataki*) often explore how mythic figures have negotiated different interests. Here are two examples:

The oricha Ochún and the oricha Oba were both married to the kingly deity Changó. Oba was unhappy because she felt that Changó spent more time with Ochún and not enough time with her. She went to Ochún and asked how she might entice Changó to pay her more attention. Ochún replied that Changó loved her cooking and that is why he spent more time with her; she also suggested that Oba make a soup from her ear because the excellent taste of the soup and the devotion of giving an ear would surely win Changó's affections. Oba made the soup and served it to Changó who commented on how good it tasted. "What is in it?" he asked. "My ear," replied Oba as she removed her head covering to reveal the bandaged ear. Changó was repulsed and fled from Oba. It is said that he never forgave her. (Ecún 1985:253)

The oricha Babalú-Ayé, the god of the earth, infectious diseases, and healing, was driven out of the land of the orichas because he was too sick. He traveled to the land of the Arará where he bathed in the first river that he found. As he bathed, a boy with smallpox arrived. Babalú-Ayé told the boy to enter the water; as the child emerged Babalú-Ayé wrapped him in a purple and white cloth and told him to return home. When the child's parents saw him they asked where he had gotten such a beautiful cloth; as the father removed the cloth, he saw that the boy no longer had smallpox. The child then told what had happened. After a time, word of the transformation spread and people came to the child for healing. Because of his success as a healer, in time, he was made the king of Arará.[8]

Thus it is clear that the orichas are not purely benevolent and universally moral subjects; like people, their interests and commitments vary depending on the time and place. But when a story is evoked via divination, the person who has come with a question or problem is expected to identify with the story and a specific character in the tale. In many stories a character will consult a diviner and make the prescribed sacrifice to ensure that all will turn out well. The client is then expected to follow through on the sacrifice prescribed by the "real-world" diviner. The story becomes a paradigm for ritual and personal action. These stories both exemplify the negotiation of interests and function as models for action in the world.

In José's case, the implications of negotiation of interests through divination are quite significant. Because he himself is a skilled diviner and "reads the shells" for himself almost every day, he constantly evaluates his commitments and negotiates resolutions for action with the spirits. Any problem can be taken to the orichas for commentary and clarification. As José once explained to me:

Para mí, es muy importante de entender todo el mundo y para ayudar a todos los demás. Y puedo ver cosas que yo no sepa, porque ésta es una capacidad para saludar a todos. Obara-Meyi dice que "No se muere él que sabe como él que no sabe."

For me it is very important to understand everyone and to help others. I can see things that I wouldn't know otherwise, because this [divination] is an ability to help everyone. The figure Obara-Meyi says, "The one who knows does not die like the one who does not know." (Velásquez 1990b)

Divination allows José to understand things that are otherwise opaque to him; this knowledge becomes a basis for wise action that improves relations with the spirits and other people.

Similarly, like all fully initiated members of Santería, José has received an itá, a detailed and lengthy divination session that is an essential aspect of the initiation rite. The itá involves reading the shells of each oricha that is received. The reading is comprehensive not only in that every deity is consulted at length but also because the past, present, and future are revealed in detail to the initiate; successive selves and subjects with different ways of being are disclosed. Similarly, taboos are established for the person; these taboos and the other information from the itá represent another important aspect of José's self-image that plays into many of his decisions about how to act in a particular situation.

Earlier in the evening, José and I went to the Maryland National Guard Armory, where he was working during the day.[9] He had left the Elegguá, the god of the crossroads and doorways, that he had made for his new godson at the workplace of warriors. Now we entered this fenced area to retrieve an essential feature of the evening's ritual. As we entered the armory, I was struck by the irony of the situation: Elegguá, the Warrior extraordinaire and touchstone of Santería dynamic vitality, was made at the National Guard Armory, stronghold of concepts of American superiority and ethnocentrism. I laughed out loud and explained to José why it seemed funny to me. "Yes," he said, "they would be surprised to know what I do here."

Here, perhaps, is the most intriguing aspect of the problem of multiple agencies and various interests. Until now I have tried to make sense of a couple of interesting moments from my fieldwork. Questions about identity are primary and followed by an exploration of the negotiations of commitments. This last incident, however, reiterates an important approach to the problem: Rather than rely solely on a semiotic, communications model to understand the various interests a person has in a given situation, it is more fruitful to explore the social construction of subjects and subjectivities—those aspects of agency that are relevant to, but not coterminous with, individual subjects. Here I point out to José a moment where two very different kinds of agency intersect in his life. He has sacrificed a chick and sung praise-songs to this newly "born" warrior Elegguá as he worked at the armory. The irony is evident to both of us as we are confronted by the differences within this singular life. José is a dedicated santero but also a janitor for the federal government. He is committed to blood sacrifice and simultaneously to keeping that commitment more or less out of sight. He has a natal family, a family of marriage, and a ritual family, all of which require attention. At any moment, at every moment, he—like the rest of us—must make choices, must negotiate which interest is the most important and which identities to exercise. Thus far, my examples have showed how personal identities, bodily patterns and gestures, and social roles are evoked, created, and negotiated. The next chapter explores how each of these aspects of experience comes together to bring forth the presence of new orichas in the initiation of a new priest.

LIVING WITH THE ORICHAS

Ritual and the Social Construction of the Deities

Rituals of sacrifice to the spirits play a critical role in Santería. Whether the sacrifice entails water poured as libations to the ancestors or the blood of a suckling goat shed for the Trickster Elegguá to transform an individual's destiny, Santería practitioners know sacrifice as a critical and efficacious form of interaction and communication with the spirits.

Rather than artificially separate sacrifice from other ritual and social interactions with supernaturals, as anthropologists and other students of religious culture have for many years, this chapter explores how Santería practitioners employ a variety of aesthetic cultural forms to constitute and sustain the social reality of the orichas. The first part explores the presence of the orichas as constituted through sacrifice in the asiento or kariocha, the most highly marked ritual in the religion, which consecrates a person as a priest or priestess of the orichas. The gods "rule" an assortment of geographical features, herbs, weather patterns, colors, animals, and actions; they also dwell in the sacred objects—stones and cowrie shells—whose consecration coincides with the making of a new santero. All these features embodying the presence of the orichas come together in the asiento. The second section lays out the formation of an interdependent relationship between priests and their orichas. After the asiento, practitioners call the new initiate by an oricha's praise-name, and the connective relationship between the initiate and the oricha takes on an individual, if public, character. The asiento gathers the oricha's presence and transfers it to the initiate. The new santero will represent the oricha in certain situations as well as act as an advocate for that oricha. Through sacrifice and a wide variety of other cultural forms, santeros continually create the orichas and reiterate their presence in the social field.

The concrete and continuous social presence of the orichas in the lives of their followers stands as a phenomenon critical to any plausible explanation or interpretation of the Regla de Ocha, as Santería is also known. The complex and compelling relationships that slowly emerge between people and divinities form one of the central arenas of oricha religious practice in West Africa and around the African Diaspora. Karin Barber, a long-time student of Yoruba culture and religion, has written about this phenomenon in the Ekiti region of Nigeria. In her estimation, "the core of the religion lies not in the public framework but in the personal bond between each devotee and the spiritual being she serves. . . . The sense of personal involvement and identification is strengthened by a feature of the religion which has been insufficiently remarked on: the multiple manifestations of 'one' òrìs[h]à" (Barber 1981:730–732).[1] In Yoruba religion, many priestesses and priests have individual shrines for their specific orichas, and thus each devotee feels that she has her "own" oricha with its specific praise-names, personality, and taboos. Just as the priestess possesses her own oricha, that oricha in turn possesses her in trance in ritual contexts, and thus their relationship is mutual. Over time, a powerful and prominent priestess will alter the way that her oricha is understood, as her personality and style will affect the oricha; "each colors the other's personality" (Barber 1981:734).

Discussing oricha practices in Oyo-Yoruba territory, Matory's powerful and insightful analysis of the tropes that organize both the rituals of initiation and the experience of being begins to account for the intensity of the relationship. Establishing the similarity between an initiate's head and the calabash that contains the oricha's consecrated objects, and exploring the containment of sacred substances, Matory demonstrates the ritual process by which the initiate is inculcated into a tightly circumscribed set of the ritual tropes that replace any previous "self" with the oricha's presence. "The ritual iconographies of . . . [orisha] worship are the material signs of the *hollow self* and the gendered nature of the subjectivity that fills it. . . . Priestly experts replace a received regime of the self with a cooperatively and locally constructed one" (Matory 1994:164). The initiate's self dissolves in the face of a collective self manufactured by the community and intimately related to the orichas.[2]

The intense and interactive relationship between priestess and divinity again emerges as a key aspect of the Candomblé and Umbanda, the Brazilian manifestations of oricha religion. Recent studies of these traditions also stress the interactive relationship. As in other places, the initiation of a priestess "consists of bringing to life in certain circumstances, or better, of resuscitating aspects of that hidden personality in the novice which correspond to the personality of the divinized ancestor. . ." (Verger 1981:44).[3] Both the initiate and the oricha have agency, but this hidden personality emerges through trance possession, a phenomenon that is not always clearly marked. So although linguistic distinctions mark which agent is acting at any given moment and seem to fix agency with one or the other of these subjects, actions performed do not always clearly implicate a single agent. As Jim Wafer writes, "It was . . . often not clear to me where the boundaries lay between spirits . . . and humans . . . , and such a boundary is necessary for agent-patient explanations of trance to be possible. I was able to use the same terminology that everyone else did to draw the necessary distinctions. But what I observed often contradicted the boundaries implied by the terminology" (1991:104). Although trance blurs those characteristics that differentiate people from the orichas, in many other contexts people's actions reinforce those differences.

THE ASIENTO: INITIATING THE PRESENCE OF THE ORICHAS

In February 1995 I traveled to Havana to attend the asiento of my friend Juan Enrique Pedroso Cálves. I met him in 1992, when he worked very hard to help my godmother organize my initiation. He pedaled all over Havana looking for the scarce and important objects for the ceremony, and many nights he would climb the stairs late in the evening, dragging his bicycle piled high with pottery basins for making medicine and bottled ingredients carefully wrapped in plastic bags to protect them. I have come out of respect and out of gratitude.

I knock on the door of the family house on Calle Bayona in Old Havana, and as soon as Juan Enrique's mother recognizes me, a commotion begins. In the house, there are ten people as well as two large cages filled with birds, four goats, and two sheep for the coming sacrifice. Once inside, I see him to the right of the door. He is dressed completely in white. He is sitting in a chair with his feet on a reed mat and faces the wall. A white towel partially covers his head. Our eyes meet and we smile as we greet each other. Awkwardly I lean down to embrace him.

"*E ku iyawó*. Greetings to the Iyawó. How are you? Are you nervous?" I ask.

"No, not really. Everything is ready, and my aunts have been preparing for weeks. How is your family?" He is allowed to get up only long enough to prostrate himself, because tonight he is doing "penance" before entering the sacred room where tomorrow he will become a priest of the fierce and majestic Changó. Even our brief exchange is unusual as he is supposed to remain silent and isolated, meditating on the new life he will soon begin. His aunt Pancha will serve as his godmother, and his aunt Norma—my godmother—will serve as his *oyubona* (Lu. one who witnesses), his second godparent. They are already preparing the great sacrifice for the coming day.

The Initiation

Key to the continuity of the Regla de Ocha, the asiento employs multiple and elaborate sacrifices to consecrate a new set of sacred objects or *fundamentos* (Sp. foundations) through which the newly initiated priestess will communicate with the orichas.[4] The ritual itself is an enormous sacrifice for the neophyte: the ceremony dedicates the remainder of her life to orichas, and it routinely costs between $5,000 and $15,000 in the United States and more than a year's salary in Cuba.[5] It unites diverse priests and priestesses, necessitates extensive ritual knowledge, and requires the performance of all the key rituals in the tradition. Secrecy shrouds the ceremony, and people with the knowledge of the proper actions and sequences as well as the reasoning behind these activities wield great power in the community. The initiation varies for each oricha, and some command many complicated preliminary ceremonies to ensure success. So important is this ceremony that a priestess's status changes after she performs her first asiento for another: before she was called *olocha* or *igüoro* (Lu. owner of the oricha, priest[ess]), and after she is known as *iyalocha* (Lu. mother of the oricha).[6] After the asiento, her orichas have given birth to new orichas, and she has given birth to her new godchild.

The ceremony itself takes seven days, not counting two days of preparatory rituals. Elders routinely say that it is impossible to understand the asiento without undergoing the ritual. However, they speak eloquently about its benefits, and every initiate has experienced the transformation it induces. Like the initiation of the Warriors, the ritual is symbolic and can be reflected upon at a discursive level, but its "deeper" meanings lie in the social and bodily experience of it. Secrecy precludes revealing too many of the details of the asiento, but it is essential to remember that much of what happens is keyed to the principal, head-ruling oricha to whom the new priest is being consecrated.

The following description reflects a generalized pattern for the ritual, a descriptive pattern found in ritual manuals published by religious practitioners (see Angarica 1955; Ecún 1985). This description reflects these generalized accounts as well as fifteen initiations in which I have participated in Cuba and the United States. It reflects the commonalities of initiations for the most common orichas: Changó, Obatalá, Ochún, and Yemayá. I have used a generalized description for two reasons: First, as mentioned, each asiento has its variations and special preparations, which do not bear on my basic point about human social activity's creating and maintaining the social presence of the orichas. Second, Santería elders do not want to make too much information available to the public, and it would be impossible for an unauthorized person to use this generalized account to generate the ritual. After adumbrating the major ritual activities of each day—activities that I have numbered in brackets for easy reference—I explicate the tropes that inform these rituals and the processes that create the orichas' presence and bind their priests to them.[7]

Every asiento requires several opening ceremonies. In most cases, two nights before the asiento proper begins, all the actors gather to perform a *misa espiritual* (Sp. spiritual mass) to receive the blessings and predictions of the egun. This ceremony begins with prayers to the good spirits that guide all present, includes songs for various categories of spirits, and can culminate in possession. Ideally, the godparents' primary ancestral spirit guides manifest, give advice to their charges, and purify the initiate. If the initiate has never been possessed by the egun, the ritual includes key segments designed to "bring down" her spirit guides. This possession by the ancestors "opens the road" for the oricha to "come down" on the first day of the asiento. Practitioners often summarize this practice by quoting the proverb *"egun lobi ocha"* or *"los muertos parieron a los orichas"* (Lu., Sp. the ancestors gave birth to the orichas).

The day before the first day of the asiento, the *oríaté* performs the *ebó de entrada* (Lu., Sp. opening sacrifice).[8] This ceremony "opens the road" for the initiation ceremony by revealing the exact nature of the spiritual circumstances at its beginning. It often includes a sacrifice to the egun or the orichas to gain their support. After this ceremony, the oyubona, the second godparent, and the initiate perform the *ceremonia del río* (Sp. ceremony of the river) [1]. Ochún, the oricha of the river, receives a sacrifice of honey and *ochinchín* (Lu. a kind of omelet). The oyubona casts four pieces of coconut to determine if Ochún has accepted the sacrifice. If she indicates that she is not content, she might advise the initiate about specific issues, or request additional sacrifices. This process continues until Ochún indicates that she has accepted the sacrifice and conferred her blessings.[9] Then the oyubona cuts away the initiate's old clothes in a ceremony called the *rompimiento* (Sp. breaking) [2]. The oyubona washes the initiate in river water. The initiate then gathers a jar of water to carry back to the initiation and a stone that will play a secret role. The ceremony of the river seeks the purification of the initiate and the blessings of Ochún, who is also responsible for joy in life.

Upon returning to the house where the initiation will take place, the oríaté realizes a small ceremony as the initiate enters the house. While the oyubona and the initiate go to the river, other priests organize the igbodú, the room where the orichas are resting and where the ritual work will be done. They decorate one corner of the room with an elaborate cloth altar—the throne—and two rows of vessels line the walls and converge in the corner. These ceramic soup tureens and wooden vessels contain the objects that will become the altars for the orichas. Each one contains a certain number of colored stones; a specific number of cowrie shells; and metal or wooden symbols that are the "tools of the oricha." The elders have selected the stones because of their color, and they have consulted each stone with the coconuts to be certain that it "eats with the oricha and the head" of the initiate [3]. The cowrie shells have been "opened"; the rounded cap is removed, so that each shell will lie flat with either its exposed interior or its serrated "mouth" facing up.

After returning to the house, the oyubona performs a rogación de la cabeza with coconut, water, chalk, cocoa butter, cotton, and two white doves. These white and pure foods strengthen the "head" of the initiate and prepare it to receive the *aché de santo* (Lu., Sp. power of the oricha) the following day. Often, the rogación will produce the first indications of spirit possession. The initiate sits in seclusion and later lies down on a woven reed mat covered with a white sheet [4]. She is betwixt and between, as if dead. No one addresses her directly, but she can do nothing alone.

The first day of the asiento itself focuses on bringing the orichas to earth in various forms and connecting their aché to the initiate. The day opens with *oro egun* (Lu. tradition of the dead). In this ceremony the community greets the spirits of the ancestors and asks for their blessing for the whole undertaking. Coconut divination again determines when the dead give their permission to proceed. The initiate is placed on a chair facing a wall and covered with a white sheet; there she does "penance" and contemplates her fate [5].[10]

The priests and priestesses retire to the igbodú, where they "sing Osain" [6] and perform the *lavatorio* (Sp. washing). The community of priests prays for the "health, luck, strength, tranquility, and spiritual evolution" of the initiate as they remove the leaves from many different herbs. They intone a series of songs to Osain,[11] the oricha of herbs, medicine, and healing, as they crush herbs and mix them with water and other ingredients to produce an osain for each oricha. Each oricha "to be born" (to be consecrated) has its own basin of osain, and the oríaté performs coconut divination before each one. A little osain is taken from each basin and given to the initiate to drink, because it "cures every sickness" (Ecún 1985:32). These osaines are then used for the lavatorio of the orichas [7]. As the priests sing praise songs for each of the orichas, they use the osaines and soap to wash the sacred objects that are becoming the mysteries of the orichas. They rinse the objects in clear water. They also rinse the cowrie shells with water and rum and then ceremonially cast them on the floor. In a notebook, a priest records the number of shells that land with the serrated "mouths" up after the name of each oricha.[12]

After this ceremony, the initiate—still covered in her white sheet—is brought to the door of the igbodú and asks for entry. She is asked what she seeks. When she responds, *"Santo,"* she is asked what oricha and must respond appropriately.[13] Although this questioning is highly ritualized in that it has a relatively fixed form and there are correct answers that are usually provided by the elders at the moment the questions are asked, this ritual underscores the initiate's free will in becoming a priestess. She asks for entry into the sacred space and explicitly requests access to the world of the orichas. From this moment on, the initiate is not called by her name but rather by the title *iyawó* (Lu.), which means younger wife [8]. As soon as she enters the room, a colored dove is sacrificed at the doorway. She must prostrate herself to her godparents. They tell the iyawó to keep her eyes closed until given permission to open them, and they remove the sheet. She kneels with her head bent over a large metal washbasin. The priests and priestesses all wash the head of the initiate, using the same osaines and same pieces of soap that they used to wash the orichas' sacred objects [9].

All the priests who are not of the same sex as the iyawó leave the igbodú. Those who remain stand the initiate up in the basin and again cut off her old clothes [10]. The priestesses wash her entire body with the cold osaines [11]. They touch a chick to the iyawó's neck, shoulders, and lower back and then slam it against the edge of the basin to kill it [12]. The basin is taken out by the youngest priest in the house, and the iyawó is dressed again in white clothes.

The other priests return to the igbodú for the *montaje del santo* (Sp. the mounting of the oricha). On the floor, the oríaté paints the "signature" of the oricha to whom the iyawó is being consecrated [13]. This *firma* (Sp.) employs the fundamental colors used to represent the full array of the orichas' power: white, red, blue, and yellow. The firma and the quantity of each color vary depending on the oricha invoked, and only oríatés know and discuss these details. On the center of this circular design, the oríaté places some of the ground herbs called aché del santo, a sum of money, and a malanga leaf [14]. A woven mat covers this, and on top of it rests an overturned wooden mortar on which the iyawó sits. On the iyawó's left wrist, a priestess places a multistrand bracelet in the colors of the principal, head-ruling oricha [15] and a simple silver manilla for Obatalá, the senior oricha of purity and creativity [16].

Then, all the elder priests and priestesses in turn take scissors, invoke all the spirits with whom they have relationships, pray for the iyawó, and cut away some of her hair [17]. They place each lock of hair in an apron made in the color of the principal oricha and worn by a priestess; this hair becomes the property of the padrino. The oyubona, the padrino, and the oríaté are the last to remove hair. The master of ceremonies finishes clearing the head of hair, soaps up the stubble, and shaves the head of the iyawó [18], while the entire assembly sings specific songs. Once the head is cleared, a priestess again performs the prayers to the head, but this time without the doves. The oríaté then paints the signature of the principal oricha on the crown of the head of the initiate [19]. Each priestess adds her blessing to this process by painting dots in the color of her oricha on the iyawó's head; thus a priestess of Yemayá paints in blue while a priestess of Obatalá paints in white. The padrino finishes this process by adding the colors of his head-ruling oricha.

Each priestess present takes a small amount of the aché de santo, invokes her spirits, prays for the iyawó, and places the aché on the center of the signature [20]. Again the oyubona and the padrino are the last to work upon the iyawó. The iyawó's head is covered with a canopy of four pieces of cloth in the four fundamental colors.

Now the *coronación* (Sp. coronation) of the iyawó begins. The oríaté with the help of two other priestesses places the godfather's Elegguá, the first divinity worked in any context, on top of the aché on the crown of the iyawó's head. The godfather's oricha is removed, and the iyawó's own Elegguá is placed on her head, as the oríaté prays to the oricha in Lucumí and for the iyawó in Spanish. The oríaté repeats this process with all the orichas present [21], and it culminates when the iyawó is crowned by her head-ruling oricha.[14] The godfather must physically crown the iyawó with the principal orichas, as the oríaté sits before her and sings praises to each oricha, pouring out as many as possible to the head oricha [22]. As he sings to the different orichas, he changes the percussive instrument he uses as accompaniment [23]. During these songs, the head-ruling oricha can possess the iyawó [24]. On those occasions when the oricha fully possesses the new priestess, the oricha can stay for an hour or so, requesting to be fed aché to facilitate speech and offering guidance to the new initiate and those present. Once the "mounting of the oricha" is completed, the padrino removes the crowning oricha, the aché de santo, and the four panels of cloth from the iyawó's head and replaces them with cotton and a white cap. The orichas now sit in an orderly line along the wall with the elder's orichas in the back and the newly born orichas in the front.

The iyawó sits in the throne and can now open her eyes. All present must prostrate themselves to the new oricha enthroned in the head of the priestess who has just been crowned [25]. The iyawó must respond by prostrating to each priestess who has helped to crown her. After a short break in the ritual action when all except the initiate eat a light meal, the assembly of priests begins the matanza. The orichas will "eat" four-legged animals and several birds according to their preferences [26]. Elegguá always eats first. He is brought to a central area with his brothers Ogún, the warrior blacksmith, Ochosi, the hunter, and Osun, the guard. Together they will share a goat and a rooster; Elegguá's brothers will also share two or three doves, whose "cool" blood is taboo for the "hot" Elegguá.[15] To prepare the sacrifice the iyawó must chew a piece of coconut and a symbolic number of guinea peppers and then spray this mass into the two ears of the animal and onto its forehead [27]. The goat's head is "presented" to the forehead, shoulders, knees, and genitals if the iyawó is male, and to the forehead and breasts if the iyawó is female.

Accompanied by specific songs in Lucumí,[16] the goat's blood covers the orichas' sacred objects [28]—those belonging to the padrino and the iyawó. The oríaté severs the goat's head and places it next to these warrior orichas. Before birds are sacrificed to the orichas, elders "present" them to the forehead, the nape of the neck, the elbows, the hands, knees, and feet of the iyawó [29]. Having finished the songs associated with the sacrifice, the oríaté leads praise songs for the feasting orichas [30]. The oríaté places salt, palm oil, and honey on the bloody base of the goat's skull, and the iyawó sticks out her tongue to taste this mixture [31]. The iyawó must pull feathers from each dead bird and sprinkle them over the sacred objects [32]. Once the sacrifice to these orichas ends, elders remove the animals and clean the room. The orichas move back to their place along the wall, and the goat's head rests on top of the oricha [33]. A priestess or the oríaté throws water on the floor where blood has spattered and feathers have fallen. The iyawó must use the feathers to clean the floor and places this feathery scrub brush in front of the orichas [34].

The sacrifice continues until the iyawó has fed each major oricha; at least five four-legged animals feed the orichas at most initiations. Once the priests and priestesses have cleaned and butchered the animals, they present the animals' most important parts (Lu. *acheces*[17]) to the oricha that consumed them; these parts include the four legs, windpipe, heart, breasts of female animals, testicles of male animals, skin, and stomach covering [35]. After this presentation, a cook prepares certain internal organs over a charcoal fire and again places them in front of the oricha [36]. After all the acheces have been presented, the oríaté performs coconut divination to determine if the sacrifice has been accepted. The iyawó is then put to bed under the throne.

Practitioners commonly refer to the following day as the *día del medio* (Sp. the middle day). Early in the morning, the oyubona bathes the iyawó, using the same herbal medicine and soap from the previous day [37]. The oyubona then repaints the firma on her head and covers the crown of the head with cotton [38]. The iyawó drinks some of the omiero, a mixture of all the osaines from the previous day, and eats a piece of coconut with a symbolic number of guinea peppers. She must also eat from the acheces that have been placed before each of the orichas.

The iyawó wears a special costume called the *traje del almuerzo* (Sp. lunch outfit), which is fashioned in gingham of the colors of the principal oricha [39]. The iyawó wears this outfit to eat a lunch consisting of a small portion of all the animals that were sacrificed the previous day [40].[18] Around noon, the iyawó changes into a lavish costume in the colors of the head-ruling oricha [41]; this costume is accompanied by the "tools" of the oricha [42]. Again seated within the elaborate "throne" altar and dressed as the head-ruling oricha, the iyawó greets visitors and well-wishers. When priests come before the iyawó dressed as her principal oricha, they must prostrate themselves to the new oricha in the head of the iyawó [43]; in turn the iyawó prostrates to the oricha in their heads. Visitors feast on the meat from the sacrifice and other foods that have been prepared for this festival day. Around six o'clock the visitors depart, the iyawó changes back into plain white clothes, and this public moment in the asiento ends.

In the morning the *día del itá* (Lu., Sp. day of history) begins with another round of baths with omiero and soap for the iyawó [44]. Again the firma is painted on the crown of the head which is then covered in cotton [45]. After the iyawó is prepared, a ceremony called *nangareo* (Lu. a food made of cornmeal and water) begins. All present go to a place where the sun is visible and offer the nangareo to the High God, called Olorun (Lu. lit. owner of heaven), to request his assistance and ask his blessing for the iyawó.

Having finished the nangareo, the collected priests return to the igbodú and begin the itá in which each oricha "born" speaks through their cowrie shell "mouths" to the iyawó about the past, present, and future. The oríaté says the *moyuba* (Lu. invocation) to call forth the spirits and asks permission to begin with the coconut oracle. Once the oricha grants permission, the oríaté hands the shells to the godfather, who in turn calls upon his spirits before handing the shells to the iyawó. With hands cupping the sacred shells, the iyawó touches her forehead, belly, and shoulders. She extends her hands to the oyubona and requests blessings. She repeats this gesture and asks the blessings of the godfather. She lowers her hands over the mat and lets the shells fall [46]. The oríaté notes the resulting first half of the divination figure, gathers up the shells, and casts them again to establish the second part. As the oricha's advice is clarified, certain spiritual matters, personal issues, and sacred directives emerge. The concerns raised here will be followed throughout the itá, as the next orichas speak to the iyawó.[19]

Before ending the consultation, the oríaté casts the shells to give a new name to the iyawó [47]. This name reflects the oricha's identity, but it will not be used for the next year. Later, however, it will become the new appellation of the priestess in all ritual contexts, whether she is greeting her orichas at home, is calling on them to assist her in healing a client, or is consulting them for guidance. The itá ends with a sacrifice either to give thanks for the blessings predicted or to clean away the negative predictions.

During the following three days, the iyawó sits in seclusion in the throne. Each morning the oyubona washes her and paints the firma on her head [48]. On the sixth day, the elders again take her before Olorun and present her newly made head to him. On the seventh day, the oyubona take the iyawó into the world. This trip often includes a visit to a Catholic church where prayers are said.[20] The trip culminates in a visit to the market, a place of social action and risk. Before encountering anyone, the elders guide the iyawó to the "four corners" of the market where she leaves simple offerings for Elegguá, the owner of the crossroads, and Oyá, the oricha of the market. The iyawó then buys and ritually steals sweet, cool fruit. She returns to the igbodú where the throne has been dismantled, and presents the fruit to the orichas. Although general taboos govern all iyawós for the first year and each priest has personal taboos from the orichas, on the seventh day the iyawó returns to the mundane world carrying new strength and new knowledge from the gods.

Social Practice and Instantiating the Orichas

To provide this strength and knowledge, the asiento repeatedly deploys a number of symbolic schemes or tropes to create the presence of the orichas. These tropes emerge in symbolic objects, ritual actions, and verbal arts, and their repetition creates an overwhelming mass of signifiers all pointing to similar but related aspects of the orichas' presence. What is this presence? How do people evoke, construct, and direct it in the asiento? And how do social practices differentiate the various orichas?[21]

It is notoriously difficult to discuss the nature and character of spiritual beings in the discourses of the human sciences. To make them manageable, folklorists and anthropologists often transform them into symbols of fundamental cultural experiences (Lienhardt 1961) or personifications of childhood traumas (Obeyesekere 1990). However, because of the importance of the orisha for Yoruba culture and society and because of emergent trends in Africanist scholarship that seek to use "indigenous" categories to explore African social life (see Mudimbe 1988), several scholars of orisha worshipers in West Africa have made forays into this difficult conceptual landscape. In 1938 William Bascom (1944:21) discussed the orishas for months with priests to establish a culturally accurate definition that stressed the ancestral role of the divinities. Robin Horton (1983) delineates the orishas' competing aspects as nature spirits and deified heroes, and Karin Barber (1981) emphasizes how orishas resemble Big Men as they compete for followers by providing their devotees with various blessings. Andrew Apter (1992:149–161) synthesizes these characteristics, claiming that orishas have all these aspects to various degrees depending on the prominence of their social following; thus the practices surrounding a lineage orisha stresses its ancestral qualities, whereas a royal orisha is most like a Big Man. Despite his erudite analytical maneuvers to explain the varying qualities of the orishas, Apter does not explore how these qualities translate into differing kinds of orisha agency or their intense presence in the lives of their devotees.

This presence has been the focus of another line of research. The term comes from the Western philosophical tradition in which presence and subjectivity are elided into a unitary and necessary prerequisite for any thought, action, or being,[22] but it has been at work in studies of African and African-based cultures for some time. William Fagg made the first important observations about presence in Yoruba culture: "[African] cultures tend to conceive things as four-dimensional objects in which the fourth or time dimension is dominant and in which matter is only the vehicle, or the outward and visible expression, of energy or life force. Thus it is energy and not matter, dynamic and not static being, which is the true nature of things" (1973:164). This energy led to Robert Farris Thompson's work (1974) on the dynamics of African art and Armstrong's detailed explorations of the "affecting presence" of Yoruba sculpture.

This affecting presence refuses to place the orishas, the artwork created for their worship, or the ritual performances enacted in that worship within a merely symbolic context. Rather than see these aspects of cultural life as reducible to cognitive and discursive meaning, Armstrong instead explores them as "purposefully concerned with potency, emotion, values, and states of being or experience—all in a clear sense powers" (1971:3–4). These powers do not stand for other things but are concrete and irreducible. In fact, they grow with time as human agents invoking presence add to them "syndetically" (Armstrong 1981:5). This work of calling forth affecting presence produces a "surplus of meaning" that cannot be contained or understood by our usual approaches to expressive culture and their emphasis on form, function, and meaning (D. Brown 1996:78–87). This "invocation" creates emotionally charged interactions between the various subjects, both the affecting and the affected.[23] The invocation of affective presence usually involves repeated interaction employing expressive cultural forms—prayers, praise songs, libations, sacrifice, and other forms of attention—but its overall affect on those involved supersedes our usual categories of analysis and points toward those slippery, nondiscursive aspects of cultural life.

Interest in the nondiscursive has become a central current in theories of social and ritual practice. Building on Mauss (1973) and Bourdieu (1989), many scholars have recently begun to explore "culture," "meaning," "society," and "tradition" as abstract reifications of the daily lived experiences and actions of creative agents—individual or corporate (see Jackson 1989). When viewed through time, these actions can be seen to "instantiate" the properties of structure that can be seen and experienced in different domains of social life (see Hardin 1993). These structural properties are never present in the same form over time but instead are brought into play by human action.[24] Thus, "structures are both constituted *by* human agency, and yet at the same time are the very *medium* of this constitution" (Giddens 1993:121).[25]

In the realm of the Regla de Ocha, then, human action by creative agents repeatedly instantiates and maintains the affecting presence of the orichas through ritual interaction.[26] One key form of interaction is sacrifice. Santeros are fond of saying *"la vida de la vida"* (Sp. life from life) to explain why washing with herbal concoctions and blood sacrifice gives life to stones, shells, and other objects. Knowledgeable practitioners transfer the vitality and power (aché) from the plants and animals to the iyawó and the sacred objects of the orichas.[27]

In the asiento, this transfer of aché is reiterated through the stones and shells, the use of herbs, the sacrifice of animals, and the singing of praise songs for the orichas. However, the ritual procedures that channel aché and instantiate the orichas also differentiate their presences. The asiento of the oricha Changó, owner of lightning and justice, has subtle differences that bring into being an aché that in turn expands and reflects, whereas the asiento of the oricha Yewá, the spiritual and solitary owner of the cemetery, instantiates a presence that retires and avoids contact with the impure. Throughout the ceremony, differences in ritual practice work to differentiate the orichas that manifest in specific contexts.

Stones

The secret and sacred objects concealed within oricha altars around the Atlantic world almost universally include stones and cowrie shells. The stones themselves come from rivers where they have been washed in rain that falls from heaven. These small stones are gathered at the river, a task usually executed by the oyubona; after being cleaned, each stone is interrogated with the coconut oracle [3]. The oracle reveals if the stone has an oricha within it, which oricha dwells there, and if that stone and its oricha "eat with the head" of the initiate. A simple initiation will require twenty-six stones each of which is asked these three questions[28]; thus the process of establishing which stones will be used requires at least seventy-eight casts of the oracle. These river stones are then placed in containers for the different orichas.

Similarly, a selection of different colors and numbers of stones further differentiates the orichas. Each oricha prefers a particular color of stone and a particular number. The stones interrogated by the coconut oracle reflect these standards. For example, Changó "takes" six or twelve black stones, Obatalá eight white stones, Ochún five yellow stones, and Yemayá seven black ones. Different colors and numbers reiterate qualities well known and closely associated with the different orichas.

The river, as the embodiment of an interaction between heaven and earth, makes an ideal spot to begin the asiento: in the ceremony of the river [1], the iyawó repeats the gathering of stones that her elders have already completed; this "secret from the river" is added to the container of the head-ruling oricha as a bit of extra aché.[29] Some practitioners maintain that the river waters transform into the small, rounded stones that most often become the indwelling sites of oricha presence (Ecún 1985: 15–16). Other practitioners stress the immortal, unchanging, and natural qualities of stones as the explanation for their use as the symbols and dwelling places for the eternal natural divinities who provide their followers with *firmeza* (Sp. steadiness, resolve). Regardless of the discursive and ideological explanations of the stones, they become the "foundation" upon which the orichas' presence rests and is built.

After the stones have been consecrated, many practitioners consider them to have life, and the discourse used to discuss and address them always posits them as living agents. Practitioners talk about the godparent's orichas "giving birth" in the asiento, and new orichas "are born." While this language might at first appear to be quaint or inconsequential, it does evidence the subjectivity that santeros ascribe to these manifestations of the orichas. In fact, santeros treasure these particular manifestations of the orichas. With the exile of many santeros, especially in the Mariel boatlift of 1980, many orichas remained in Cuba separated from their priests. While many santeros consecrated new stones to reconstitute their oricha altars, they continue to place great emotion and value on the stones that "went to the head" in the asiento. This fact underscores two important qualities of these orichas. First these original orichas have been intimately connected to the spiritual head of their priest in an inalterable process of crowning [21] (to which I return later). Second, as the long-time receptacles of greetings, prayers, moyubas, attention, songs, and sacrifice, these particular stones as manifestations of the orichas have more presence than newly sanctified stones do. Because practitioners consider them to have more presence, the elder orichas have more aché, act more effectively, and provide superior guidance than their younger counterparts.

Shells

This guidance comes through the next critical element in the fundamento: cowrie shells.[30] Before the asiento begins, the oyubona "opens" cowries by creating a hole in the rounded back of the shells, inserting a scissor blade, and popping off the back. This process produces shells that, when cast, will land with the serrated "mouth" either up or down. After opening shells, the oyubona adds a "hand of shells" to the stones of each oricha. Elegguá receives twenty-one to match the number of his manifestations or "roads" (Sp. *caminos*), whereas most other orichas receive eighteen. These elders wash and feed the shells with the stones of the orichas, and each oricha will speak through sixteen shells to the initiate. After the asiento, the initiate will guard these shells for the rest of her life as the "mouth of the orichas."

This expression underscores the most critical and universal understanding of the cowrie shells' role in the religion. Practitioners routinely say that the orichas speak to their followers through these shells. That practitioners refer to the shells as the mouths of the orichas likens the orichas to people and reiterates their agency. The orichas, like people, speak. Whether through the shells [46] or through the lips of an oricha who has possessed a priestess [24], the oracular speech of the orichas plays an important role in the individual lives of practitioners. In the itá, the orichas provide baseline advice to the initiate about ideal goals to pursue and challenges that she will face. In more general readings or through possession, the orichas often address a particular problem and prescribe a specific animal sacrifice or a cleaning with a particular herb.

Herbs

Herbs (Lu. *ewes*, Sp. *hierbas, yerbas*) associated with specific orichas contain particularly intense aché and their ritual manipulation often instantiates the orichas. All orichas are "born" by being washed in the herbal liquid called osain and then "fed" with animal blood. Practitioners use two explanations to refer to this process. Some say, "Nothing is born without water and blood." In this model of the asiento, the birth of the oricha follows the birth of a human being; the water breaks and then blood flows as the new life emerges. Other santeros say that orichas are born in the "cool" water and "fed" with "warm" blood.[31] Here the herbal water again echoes the water of human birth, but the sacrifice strengthens the orichas.[32] In either case, herbs mixed with water provide some of the vitality necessary to bring a new oricha into being.[33]

The first day of the initiation begins with "singing Osain" [6]. In this ritual the assembled santeros mix herbs, water, smoked ground fish and *jutía* (Sp. a large rodent[34]), palm oil or cocoa butter, honey or molasses, chalk, various kinds of alcohol, and guinea peppers[35] while singing praise songs to Osain.[36] One song for Osain that is regularly performed at the asiento links the themes of herbal vitality to the immortal qualities of stone already discussed: *O yiki yiki ota l'omí o!* (Lu. the stone in the water is immortal, o!). Like the immortal stone, herbs provide access to the regenerative life of orichas.

The herbs and other ingredients used in the osaines vary somewhat depending on the oricha. Each oricha "owns" certain herbs, and the osain will contain a predominance of herbs belonging to the head ruling divinity. For example, Yemayá "owns" ferns and water lettuce, plants associated with wet areas appropriate to the divinity of the sea; these two herbs would be present in her asiento, and priestesses would be certain to place a good deal of these leaves into the basin for Yemayá. Knowledgeable practitioners always require certain herbs for the osaines at an asiento, and each of these special herbs "has" its own power. Practitioners gloss these different qualities as follows: *Bledo blanco* provides dignity and seniority; *peregún* transforms the life of the iyawó; and *wereyeye* preserves that life.[37]

In addition to herbs, osaines include other ingredients as well. Most orichas' osaines take palm oil. Obatalá and Ochosi take cocoa butter instead; these same two orichas also take *cascarilla* (Sp. white chalk made from eggshell), and Obatalá takes no alcohol. Most osaines include honey, but those belonging to Yemayá and Elegguá take molasses, which is their preferred sweetener. Guinea pepper is always the last ingredient added to the osaines, and all the orichas receive their symbolic number of peppercorns. Although santeros can provide a whole range of mythic tales and other explanations for these differences, they function to differentiate the osaines and the instantiated character of the various orichas washed in the osaines [7].

This differentiated instantiation also exists in the other major herbal component of the asiento, the aché de santo. The night before the montaje del santo, the oyubona takes Oké, the oricha of the hill who is associated with stability and immortality, and grinds a few leaves from each of the herbs to be used in the asiento. Again, this mixture will have herbs that belong to all the orichas but will include a majority that belong to the head-ruling oricha. To this paste she adds four seeds that are also referred to as aché de santo: *obí* (Lu. coconut), *eru* (Lu. a kind of pepper), *osun* (Lu. camwood), and *kola* (Lu. red kolanut). Without the diversity of herbs for the orichas and these critical seeds, the aché de santo would be incomplete.

When applied to the signature of the oricha both on the floor under the iyawó [13, 14] and on the crown of her head [19, 20], this herbal formula transforms the initiate by consecrating her to the head oricha and making possession by that oricha more possible and safe. Like the stones and the osaines, the aché de santo contains different ingredients to "give birth" to various oricha presences.

Blood

After the orichas have come to life through the osaines' aché and the initiate has received the aché de santo, the large-scale blood sacrifice begins [26, 28].[38] This sacrifice routinely involves the ritual slaughter of five four-legged animals and a retinue of twenty-five birds: It creates an "unforgettable and impressive" experience, as an uninitiated practitioner said to me in 1992.

Within the religion, most practitioners understand this sacrifice to be a direct transference of the life of the animal to the life of the orichas. Through sacrifice the aché of the orichas is strengthened. On several occasions I have witnessed strong young goats resisting sacrifice. As they struggled, oríatés commented, *"Mira esa fuerza que ya tiene el oricha"* (Sp. see that strength that the oricha now has).[39] In the asiento, the animals' vitality plays a critical role because the godparent's orichas have just "given birth" and the iyawó's have just been born. At this crucial and dangerous moment, the godparent's and iyawó's orichas "eat" together in a communal feast. This ebó will reinforce the strength of the parental orichas and ideally please and nourish the newborn orichas before they speak to the iyawó during the itá.

Pleasing the gods requires knowledge of their individual tastes and histories. All the orichas have a particular four-legged animal that they must eat in the asiento, and with these animals they eat their favorite birds [26]. Just as Elegguá "eats" goat and rooster with his brothers, the Warriors, other orichas "eat" together. The orichas share together at the level of ritual practice, but this ritual detail usually indexes some mythic explanation as well. Ochún and Aganyú share castrated goat, and santeros explain this fact by pointing to their strong association with the river; they are of the same place and eat the same food. Yemayá and Changó routinely share their sheep, roosters, and guinea hens; for santeros, this ritual reality reflects their intense mother-son relationship. Conversely, Yemayá has never forgiven Oyá for breaking up Changó's relationship with Oba, and neither Yemayá nor Oyá eats while the other is present. These practical differences in the sacrifices offered to various orichas and the myths that sometimes explain them both help bring into being the differences in the orichas themselves.

These differential blood sacrifices end the most significant process of bringing the orichas to life through repeated, additive activities. Throughout the asiento the orichas have been "called" through prayers [6, 20, 22, 30] and praise songs that enhance their presence. In the Regla de Ocha as in Yoruba culture, words carry the power to create conditions of reality.[40] Priests chant these praise songs during the singing of Osain as the orichas are washed [7]. Each oricha is again praised through song when the iyawó is crowned [22]. While the principal oricha rests on the aché de santo on the iyawó's head, the oríaté serenades all the orichas, playing their favorite instruments; this process invokes the orichas into the iyawó's head at the same time that it differentiates him or her from other orichas. Again, during the blood sacrifice, the collected priests chant the oricha's praises [30]. After the sacrifice of the blood, the four-legged animals' heads end up resting atop their respective orichas' containers [33]. After the butchering of the animals, elders again present key body parts to the gods [35], cook the internal organs, and place these in front of the orichas [36]. All these activities focus on the orichas and build up their presence in the life of the iyawó.

Throughout the asiento priests add "cool" herbs and "hot" blood to the stones and shells of the orichas, building affecting presences on these foundations. For Armstrong, affecting presences have the "powers" of creativity, subjectivity, and particularity (1981:19). The newborn orichas of the iyawó result from the procreativity of the godparent's orichas. They have agency and individuality created and sustained through ritual and differentiated through stones, herbs, animals consumed, and songs performed. Their individuality results from the ways in which the priestesses and the iyawó enact their relationships and perform their obligations to them. Thus, as Anthony Giddens might say, the orichas are both constituted *by* human agency, and yet at the same time are the very *medium* of this constitution. Santería practitioners instantiate the orichas; in turn, the gods and their priests exist in ongoing, "enacted" relationships that sustain their mutual presence (Armstrong 1981:19, 27).

INSTRUMENTS OF THE ORICHAS: CONNECTIVE RELATIONSHIPS BETWEEN THE ORICHAS AND THEIR PRIESTS

The presence of the orichas and their priests emerges from sustained and performed relationships that begin at the asiento when the orichas and the iyawó are "born." The asiento not only instantiates the newborn orichas and reinforces the older pantheon, but it also transforms the subjectivity of the initiate. Several sets of imagery convey this change and saturate the ritual with repeated tropes. The first and arguably most powerful trope alludes to the rebirth of the initiate.[41] Another set of images reiterates the royalty of the orichas to impress both the initiate and the community with the power, prestige, and presence of the orichas. Another trope treats the whole event as a marriage of the initiate to the head oricha to constitute communicatively the intimate relationship between the iyawó and the head oricha. This initiation ritual—like so many rites of passage—follows the classic tripartite structure of separation, liminal transition, and reintegration in the social world, but it is these specific tropes that differentiate it from others.

Abokú: *Rites of Separation*

The asiento begins with ceremonies to separate the initiate from her previous life, and the images at play in these rituals culminate in the symbolic death of the initiate. The first day of the asiento proper includes several ceremonies that underscore the removal of the initiate from her normal surroundings. In the ceremony of the river [1], the godparents take the initiate to a river, literally cut off her clothes in the rompimiento [2], and cast them into the streaming water to be carried away forever. Two interpretations of these events circulate among priests. The simpler explanation maintains that this ritual cleans away the previous life and identity of the initiate. The old clothing represents the old life that is cast away, and thus this ceremony begins the process of rebirth by "erasing" (Sp. *borrar*) the past. A more nuanced interpretation informed by extensive references to the mythological underpinnings of the rituals maintains that these ceremonies reenact the first asiento in which the first iyawó—Ibá Omí—disappeared in the river.[42] In either case the ceremony of the river represents the first ritual of separation.

After this ceremony the initiate is no longer called by her previous, secular name. In many houses she is called *abokú* (Lu. one who worships death); in other houses she is called iyawó from this moment. In either case, this name change further separates her from her previous identity. Not only is she not called by her own name, but she is also addressed by a title, a social marker that many others have used before her. The individual begins to dissolve into the traditionally established social roles.

This erasure of the individual continues with other images made concrete in the ceremony. Following the ceremony of the river, the initiate spends the night laid out on a mat covered by a white sheet [4], just as a corpse does. Early on day two of the asiento, the initiate is covered with a white sheet and is placed in a corner to do penance [5], just as the body of a deceased person is shrouded in white cloth. Throughout these procedures the initiate lacks agency and name; she cannot eat or talk. After entering the sacred room to begin the mounting of the orichas, elders again cut away her clothes [10]. Someone bludgeons a chick to death on the side of the washbasin, just as a survivor slams a young chicken against the floor in the funeral of a priest. This ceremony reiterates the rompimiento of the ceremony of the river but with a difference: Here the initiate is separated from her status as an abokú and begins her new life. The harshness of the chicken's death reminds all present that these transitions never come easily.

Soon thereafter the elders cut away the initiate's hair [17] and shave her head bare [18] in preparation for the new life she will undertake. The ritual removes her hair—her public persona, her self-presentation—and clears all traces of past growth. The cutting and removing of hair further underscore her separation from her past. Through repeated ritual actions, initiators remove symbols and icons of the initiate's old life and identity. Severing her from her old life makes her ready to start a new one.

Making Oricha Is Making a King: Liminality and Communitas

After the many images of death have enveloped the initiate, the royal and nuptial metaphors intermix and govern the next phases of the asiento. These processes identify the new initiate with the orichas in general and the head-ruling oricha in particular. In many ways, the initiators treat the body of the initiate and the orichas' sacred objects in identical ways to underscore that each will serve as vessels for the gods. Omiero and soap wash and purify the orichas on the first day of the asiento [6, 7], and the same sacred herbs and the same soap wash the new priest on that day and each of the following days of the asiento [9, 11, 37, 44, 48]. Both the sacred stones and the body of the initiate must be purified, "cooled," and empowered by the aché of the herbs, so that they can contain the power of the orichas.

Just as the orichas' sacred containers "wear" beaded necklaces, the elders place a colored, beaded bracelet [15] and a silver manilla [16] on the left wrist of the initiate. Many practitioners know that these beads once marked the exclusive power and prestige of Yoruba kings, and they proudly display their beads to remind themselves and others of their own royal status as priests of the orichas. The beaded *idé* (Lu. bracelet) reflects the colors associated with the head-ruling oricha, and the manilla belongs to Obatalá, the cool and benevolent father of the orichas. Both bracelets socially differentiate initiated priests from the uninitiated, and the symbolism of these status-marking bracelets suggests that every action of the new initiate also implies and implicates the oricha of the head and Obatalá. Like Obatalá, the initiate should only touch the world with tranquility and wisdom.

The colors of the idé often reiterate and augment the colors of the stones used to represent and differentiate the oricha presences. Not only do these colors sometimes appear in the stones and the bracelet, but they also appear on other key objects in the ceremony to emphasize further the presence of .the orichas. Ochún takes yellow with hints of green and red. Changó takes red and white. Yemayá takes shades of blue with white. Obatalá takes white with other colors to accent it. The tureens that contain the orichas' objects reflect these colors, just as the *collares de mazo* (Sp. multistrand necklaces) include colors that help instantiate the different orichas; these large necklaces are draped over the tureens on altars and over the initiate's shoulders on the middle day of the asiento. Similarly, the initiate's clothing reflects the colors associated with the orichas. The gingham lunch outfit [39] includes the central color of the oricha in contrast with white.[43] The gala royal clothing of the middle day also reflects these colors [41], as do the implements that initiates carry to embody the oricha's powers and capacities [42].[44]

These colors also appear in precise patterns in the head oricha's signature (Sp. *firma*). Painted on the floor beneath the initiate [13] and repeatedly on the crown of her head [19, 38, 45, 48], the firma's form and colors vary from oricha to oricha. The basic form includes several concentric circles with an open space in the center that receives the herbal aché [13, 14, 19, 20], and different religious families also continue to use variations to distinguish themselves from others. The firma always functions to call the oricha to possess a follower. Both on the floor beneath her and on her head, the firma's colors and the aché further identify the initiate with the head-ruling oricha.

This ceremony begins the process of the "coronation," where royal metaphors rule the ceremonial action. On top of the aché on the head, the elders gather around the initiate and crown her with the tureens that contain the sacred objects of the orichas [21] while the master of ceremonies calls out to the gods with praise songs. These "crowns" enhance the individual person's presence, and to receive them, she must, for a moment at least, become the very center of attention in her community. The middle day's ceremonies repeat this process when the initiate appears dressed in gala royal garb and receives the wider community [41]. This social structure reflects a king surrounded by subjects without whom he would not be a ruler.

If the initiate rules over a community, the orichas literally stand above the initiate. This physical action underscores the fact that the initiate's life will now be under the control and guidance of the orichas. Some refer to this ceremony as the "mounting" of the oricha, and it often culminates in full possession. Kingly and nuptial metaphors unite here, as the regal orichas rest on the initiate's head and "mount" (Sp. *montar*) her in possession.[45] In some religious houses the oríaté opens the initiate's head with a small cruciform incision to the crown; this opening allows the aché to penetrate the physical barrier of the initiate's body just as the oricha will penetrate it in possession. In possession, the oricha takes (Sp. *coger*) the initiate—an expression whose sexual meaning translates perfectly between English and Spanish. These sexual tropes always inscribe the initiate as having little or no agency in relationship to the oricha: she is iyawó [8], the younger wife of the oricha, dependent on the head oricha for her status, situation, and agency. For a year the new initiate is called only *iyawó*, thus distancing her even more from her previous identity and reinforcing the agency of the oricha. In the asiento the oricha's agency becomes most obvious as she is eclipsed by her metaphorical husband in possession. All the work of separation is completed. For a time the oricha visits the elder priestesses who have worked so hard to summon the powers. Ironically, the iyawó, though the physical center of this community, becomes psychically absent; possession wipes out the consciousness of the possessed and usually leaves no memories of what has occurred.

After the possession has ended and the oricha departed, the iyawó sits within the cloth altar. The community of priests now includes the iyawó, and each prostrates before her to honor the oricha that now dwells in her head; the iyawó in turn prostrates to show her respect for the orichas that have helped bring her oricha into the world [25]. This same series of mutual prostrations repeats on the middle day when the iyawó wears the royal garb of the oricha [43].

However, before the iyawó can sit as the enthroned oricha, she must undergo further subjugation to the orichas by being repeatedly identified with the animals that are sacrificed to them. The elders "present" all the animals to the iyawó [29]. This presentation physically touches each animal to and thus identifies it with the initiate. By chewing coconut and guinea pepper and then spraying the resulting mass onto the head of the four-legged animals [27], the iyawó makes physical the movement of her prayers. The coconut and pepper embody her prayers and move to the heads of the animal; its blood then covers the oricha. The iyawó must taste blood from the base of the four-legged animals' skulls and so further associates herself with the animals sacrificed to the orichas [31]. The animals' heads ultimately rest on top of the oricha [33], as do the feathers that the iyawó pulls from each dead bird and sprinkles over the sacred objects [32]. The iyawó cleans the floor with some of the feathers and places them in front of the orichas [34]. In each of these cases, the iyawó physically relates to the animals that are feeding the orichas, animals being sacrificed to change the life of the initiate. The implications of this identification have deep ramifications for the iyawó: she will sacrifice herself to the orichas for the rest of her life.[46] In return for these ongoing offerings she will receive the blessings of the orichas.

In the itá [46], the orichas each speak to the iyawó about "the past, present, and future." The head-ruling oricha speaks last and reveals the iyawó's essence. The divination figure given by the head oricha provides a canonical set of proverbs, stories, prayers, and sacrifices with which the iyawó will improvise for the rest of her life. When first meeting, practitioners often ask, "What figure do you have on your head?" Many practitioners go to great lengths to protect this information as it reveals their weaknesses. In discussing the head odu, Margot Torres, a senior priestess of Oyá, said, "The figure on your head is what you are and how you react and what you do. It tells you everything about a person."

Using this divination figure as a starting point, the oríaté asks the head oricha to give a new name to the iyawó [47]. These names often refer to the qualities of the divination figure and the head oricha. For example, an iyawó of Yemayá, the oricha of the ocean, usually has *omí*, the Lucumí word for water, in her name; a priestess with great blessings from Yemayá might be called Omí Bemí, meaning "water benefits me." Similarly, priestesses of Changó, the royal oricha of thunder, almost always carry names including the word *obá* (Lu. king),[47] suggesting that his priestesses should see themselves as extensions of his royalty. These names not only link the individual to the head oricha symbolically but also suggest certain oricha qualities for them to emulate. Each priestess carries an individual name that constitutes one aspect of her connection to her head oricha.

The itá allows the orichas to speak through the voices of the community to the iyawó about appropriate conduct. Although the odus do have certain objective qualities—like proverbs, standardized advice, and allegorical stories—the *italero* leading the ceremony and the gathered community express the specific meaning of these aspects of the odu and their relevance for the initiate. Here the iyawó may reveal or confess private concerns, but the orichas—socially mediated by the elders present—place the sanctions on her behavior. This process echoes the naming of the initiate, because the iyawó is again identified with the orichas. The head-ruling oricha speaks, and the elders refer to the advice given again and again. At a psychological level the head oricha's character usually reflects significant aspects of the initiate's personality. The itá then results in an auto-apotheosis, which objectifies certain aspects of the initiate's personality through the orichas and directs her how best to manifest these qualities in the outer world. These behaviors include all aspects of life: career choices to be made, religious performance traditions to master, family relationships to nurture or transform, and matters of the heart to weigh. Any questions about behavior can be clarified through yes-or-no questions or through later consultations.

Connectivity

The identification of the initiate with the head oricha in the asiento results in the slow merging of their personalities and social faces in the years following the initiation. The standard characteristics of the head oricha become increasingly visible in the social actions of the priestess. These qualities become fluid parameters for the identity of the initiate, as do the constant exchanges back and forth between the oricha and the priestess. Some practitioners maintain that the priestess remains herself and uses her older name under normal circumstances, but becomes an "instrument of

the orichas" called by their names when engaged in working with the deities.[48] Such clear delineations, however, remain elusive for most practitioners: Stereotypes about the different orichas' priestesses and blurring the
lines of agency both underscore the fluidity of the relationship. These stereotypes based on the well-known stories about the divinities emerge for
each of the orichas and their initiated "children."[49] For example, Ochún's
children are stereotypically considered full of themselves, gregarious, im-
patient, and fun-loving. Obatalá is thought to be serious—even ponderous,
gentle, intelligent and wise, and extraordinarily confident. His priestesses
usually share these characteristics; a priestess of Oyá once told me of an
Obatalá priest she knew, "He is a great diviner but like all Obatalás, his
head swells sometimes." Even this reference to "a child of Obatalá" as an
"Obatalá" constitutes the intimate connection between orichas and their
priests but also reveals the blurring of categories of subjectivity.

The question of agency in working the orichas again points to integral
and changing relationships between orichas and their priests. The daily
life of many oricha priests includes spiritual problem-solving for individual clients. When a client comments on the specificity of the divination
reading, priestesses are fond of saying, *"Los orichas no mienten"* (Sp. the
orichas do not lie); this phrase emphasizes the agency of the orichas in de-
tailing the client's situation and downplays the extensive talent and training a priestess must possess to become a skilled diviner. After an offering
or sacrifice has changed a difficult situation, clients often thank priests for
their assistance, and the priests' responses vary; the commonly heard
phrase *"Maferefún oricha"* (Lu. praise be to the orichas) suggests that the
orichas were the agents responsible for the change in the situation. Another frequently used expression refers to the head-ruling oricha as *"muy
grande"* (Sp. very great), highlighting the importance of the oricha to
whom they are most intimately connected.

These common expressions all blur the lines between the actions of the
orichas and the actions of their priests and thus point to the connective relationships that exist between these different agents. In a connective relationship the two parties see themselves as part of one another. The
boundaries between the agents remain relatively fluid, so that each requires the presence of the other to round out a sense of complete identity
(see Keller 1986; Minuchin, Rosman, and Baker 1978). The priestess's
sense of her own subjectivity rests on her intimate relationship to the
oricha's subjectivity such that the security, identity, integrity, dignity, and
self-worth of the priestess are tied to the actions of the oricha. Because

priestesses live in connective relationships with the orichas, the priest-esses' actions affect the orichas: practitioners believe that satisfied orichas bless their priestesses by giving them "health, luck, strength, tranquility, and spiritual evolution" and providing them with the aché to heal others through ritual and prayer. However, displeased orichas "flog" their priestesses with many misfortunes, including "loss, tragedy, illness, and death." The priestess does not exist when separated from the oricha; she cannot be autonomous. She requires the presence of the oricha to shape her emotions, desires, attitudes, and subjectivity.[50]

The key to the Regla de Ocha lies in the complex and compelling per-sonal bond between the orichas and their individual followers. To consti-tute fully the presence of the head-ruling oricha in a person's life requires the extensive and elaborated ritualizing of the asiento and its many atten-dant sacrifices. This ritualizing transforms the individual subjectivity of each priestess through the creation of a permanent relationship with her head-ruling oricha. Once instantiated by the work of sacrifice and con-nected to the individual in the asiento, the orichas become integral to the sense of individual and social identities of their followers. As Santería priestesses and priests spend their lives in ongoing interaction and mutual identification with their head-ruling orichas, intimate and definitional re-lationships emerge—a lived experience that the clinical psychological lan-guage of connective relationships begins to describe. Through time these relationships become increasingly charged with affect, desire, and power. But how do priests and priestesses understand and use the ritual and social power of the gods in their daily lives?

IMAGINING POWER

The Aesthetics of Aché in Santería

The March sun heats my shoulders as I lock my Chinese bicycle to an iron fence in a dead-end street in downtown Havana. It is 1995. I have come to the house of a senior *babalawo* (Lu.), a priest of the oricha Orula and practitioner of the Ifá divination system. He is well connected to the thriving black market in the city, and I have come to change money. The priest and his wife, who is a priestess of Yemayá, the oricha of the ocean, are famous for their knowledge of Santería. Since the early 1960s they have spent their time helping people with their problems and initiating them into the religion. I have been coming to their house for three years.

After knocking on the peeling paint of the double door, I hear a voice calling me from the balcony above. It is Luisa, the priestess.[1]

"*¿Quién es?*" she asks in her loud, gruff voice as she squints in the morning sun. "Who is there?"

"Good morning. It's Michael. How is it going today?"

"Orestes isn't here, but I will come down and let you in," she says as she disappears from behind the iron grill of the balcony. After a long moment, the lock on the blue double door cries out and the right door groans. Luisa tells me to enter. I follow her up the narrow steps. The walls at the landing are marked with tire tracks from the many bicycles that have made this same journey. At the top of the stairs, Luisa tells me to sit on the couch. In front of me is a large statue of Our Lady of Caridad del Cobre, the patron saint of Cuba, who is associated with the oricha Ochún, who "is the river and love and all the good things in this life."[2] The statue is faded blue, and the head of the virgin is dusty.

"Orestes told me he could help me change some dollars into pesos," I say. "Yes, he knows people. He will help you, but I don't know when he will return. It shouldn't be too long. Want some water?" "No, thanks," I say. With this, Luisa moves to the balcony. She looks at the sky and sucks her teeth. I have seen this before. I think I know what is coming.

Luisa is a strong-willed woman, but after almost forty years with the forceful Orestes, she is often quiet. She usually lets him do the talking, but in his absence things are different. With no introduction, she begins to tell me a story:

"A few years ago, the old man and I went to Venezuela to do some work. We were going to make Yemayá to one of his godchildren in Ifá.[3] We did the spiritual mass and worked the egun. We went to the river and we did the cleaning. It was the day of the matanza, and we were in the room [where the secret ritual work is done]. I was the oyubona (Lu. second godparent), and the oríaté had started the osain. But when he handed me the herbs, I asked him where the peony and the peregún were." Luisa crosses the room and leans against the door to the room where her orichas live.

"He said, 'We couldn't find them around here.' I had been watching what was happening up until then. I had noticed that these herbs were missing. But I was the oyubona, I was responsible for what was happening, so I said, 'You can't do it without these leaves. The godparents have to add peony and peregún to the osain.' He objected, but after a while we got a car and drove a couple of hours and found the plants we needed so that we could continue."

Luisa moves back to the balcony. The sun lights up her face, and her eyes remain steady, fixed on something far away. These stories always have a point and I am pretty sure Luisa will let me know what it is. "To have aché you must have three things. You must have a conscience, you must have obedience, and you must be human. You can't make an oricha without peony and peregún, and so I stopped the ceremony right in the middle. I made him get those herbs before we continued." As the conversation continued, Luisa explained what she meant by conscience, obedience, and being human. A person with conscience does what she knows is right, she follows tradition, and she acts responsibly and righteously. A person with obedience listens to the orichas and the egun and follows their directions. A person is human when she defends other people's interests, when she fights for justice, and when she is compassionate and generous. "To be a good santero, to have aché, you have to have conscience, obedience, and be human." Although we go on talking for a couple more hours about the history of the religion, the esoterica of ritual, and family events of the past few years, this story about aché is what I keep thinking about.

IDEAS ABOUT GENERATIVE POWER

A senior priestess, who is usually reserved, addressed an ethnographer, a business associate, and a younger priest. She chose to speak of a key concept in the religion and to explain what kinds of people have power, talent, character, and competence. Her story situates her as a person with aché. She is capable, powerful, and knowledgeable, and she acts with conscience, in obedience to the tradition, and in the interest of her godchild. The priestess has shown herself acting forcefully and dynamically in a ritual setting, and in the process she has adumbrated and embodied the characteristics of a person with aché.

In Santería, everyone has ideas about aché: what it is, how it works, and how to get it. Opinions abound because most practitioners agree that ritual manipulates aché to assist people in resolving their difficulties and obtaining their goals. This power is present in all objects, plants, animals, and humans, but it is concentrated in priests and priestesses of the orichas and in the orichas themselves. By bringing together the correct substances and the correct supernatural forces, ritual transforms people's circumstances in the world. At the level of the individual, aché allows people to act with force, intelligence, and impunity. Most practitioners consider this power to be both innate and augmented by behavior and ritual. People will say of a gifted diviner, "He has an aché for divining"; thus the term can also refer to a particular talent that a person has. When someone offers an inspired interpretation of a ritual situation or performs well, santeros respond by saying, "*Aché pa' ti*" (aché for you); here aché is offered as a high compliment and an honor conferred by others who have power, talent, and knowledge. Aché causes curses to take effect and gives solace to the suffering. Still, this key concept is quite variable.[4] No two santeros ever give the same explanation of aché; instead aché is *imagined* differently by different actors.

As actors working the notions of aché they have received in their training, santeros have extremely varied sources for their social knowledge of ritual power. In Cuba and other places where the religion thrives, many forces have shaped the practice of the Regla de Ocha. Historically, Santería has been defined as a paradigmatic syncretic religion. The common wisdom has been that enslaved Yoruba were brought together on sugar plantations and in urban areas where, with the assistance and at the behest of the civil and church authorities, they formed *cabildos* (Sp. mutual aid societies) where they mixed Cuban-style Roman Catholicism with the "traditional" beliefs of the Yoruba (cf. Brandon 1993:55–103; Ortiz 1984; Argüelles Mederos and Hodge Limonta 1991:35–83). The most obvious example of this syncretism is that the orichas were "worshiped" in the form of Catholic saints. According to the accepted history, Spiritism arrived from France in the nineteenth century and was also mixed with these practices and reconciled with them. In addition to Santería, Cubans also practiced two other "syncretic" religions with distinct ethnic origins: Palo Mayombe, also called Palo Monte, from the Kongo of Central Africa, and Abakuá from the Efik and Ejagham of the Cross River delta in Nigeria. Because of Cuban cultural politics extant since the turn of the century, it has often been convenient, if not necessary, for practitioners of these religions to engage the discourse of anthropology and label themselves "syncretic" from time to time (see Palmié 1995).[5]

Putting aside the difficulties of static concepts such as *tradition* and the fact that Santería practitioners very rarely use the verb *worship* when describing their religious activities,[6] this history has other problems. Recent research has showed the limited historical and demographic impact of the cabildos in Havana and elsewhere in the colonial period. Santería is the most widespread of the Afro-Cuban religious traditions, but historical records show that very few cabildos were labeled with the Afro-Cuban ethnonym Lucumí. Thus the number of cabildos of any given ethnicity cannot be taken to imply any specific level of cultural influence (López Valdés 1995). Similarly, following the lead of Bastide's research in Brazil on religious institutions and knowledgeable practitioners (1978), research on the history of the Regla de Ocha has showed the relative importance of specific priestesses and priests born in Africa to the growth and contemporary form of the religion. In the Ifá tradition, all babalawos trace their spiritual ancestry to five known practitioners who were active in the late nineteenth and early twentieth centuries (D. Brown 1995). Similarly, knowledgeable practitioners describe current ritual forms as influenced greatly by the famous reformer Efuché, a priestess born and trained in Africa, who arrived in Cuba in the early twentieth century, at least fifteen years after abolition (Pichardo 1994). This history makes clear that the contemporary structure of Santería did not result from some indiscriminate and vague syncretic process, but rather from individual practitioners acting upon their lifeworlds.[7]

In my own research, I have come across many references to a tome published in the 1940s that codified the Regla Kimbisa. This tradition was a revitalization movement that attempted to merge the three most prominent Afro-Cuban religions with astrology and numerology (Cabrera 1977), and the book to which so many of my associates refer compiled and integrated ideas, rites, and attitudes from these disparate traditions. Even today practitioners will invoke this book to authenticate a claim or a ritual detail. From these examples it should be clear that no history of this religion can be easy or straightforward.

Practitioners act on ideas and enact rituals that they have culled from a huge variety of sources. The extent of the mixing between Santería and other traditions is never fixed and is often opaque. Because the source of religious ideas and practices is never clear and because the tradition is reproduced through time, syncretism merely names a standard aspect of all cultural processes in which different systems of meaning-making are reconciled to some degree. Instead of discussing Santería within the context of a mixing with other traditions, it is more edifying to begin with the agency of practitioners. Though it might be misleading to say that Santería itself is a syncretic tradition, an admixture of other traditions, it is accurate to say that many practitioners of the religion are syncretic in their approach to their religious activities.[8] As the individuals reproduce the tradition, it has changed and continues to change. Santería practitioners—like all people—constitute and work on their world through a variety of structures and systems of meaning. Careful attention to their actions, and to explanations of those actions, can provide a portrait of the creativity of social power and performative competence in a single community (see Arens and Karp 1989; Bauman 1989).[9]

IMAGINING ACTION

By focusing on practitioners' accounts of aché, on their actions, and on their evaluations of other people, this chapter focuses on the details of cultural life in a particular time and place and explores how ritual, as a communicative and socially constitutive process intended to affect the flow of power in the universe, is a context in which people can respond to the contradictions and tensions engendered by social and cultural change (see Bauman 1989 and Comaroff and Comaroff 1993). After exploring how aché is imagined by several different practitioners, the chapter examines how these notions of ritual power structure action, how they are used to evaluate the actions of others, and how these notions are deployed in social life to gain authority. Here I want to lay out the key elements that Santería practitioners use to understand and act on the world in the religion. I will outline certain principles, but this approach should not be construed to suggest that the ideal is in any way primary. Rather, these basic beliefs are only a part of the cultural practices that constitute the Regla de Ocha.

In recent years, practice theorists and other scholars have returned to key questions in social theory and in particular have focused on the critical symbolic and social structures with which actors address their circumstances (e.g., Comaroff 1985). As anthropologists and others have struggled to understand the pluralistic universe, several approaches have emerged to address the difficult nexus of individual agents and the symbolic and social structures with which they apprehend the world and their actions. We have seen a parade of academic discourses since the turn of the century: William James's pragmatism,[10] functionalist universalism, modes of thought, symbol mediation, and practice theory. These disparate schools share an interest in the external and objective realities of social and cultural structures as well as the internal and subjective experience of individual agents. Building on Emile Durkheim's insight that ritual connects the individual imagination to the collective through communicatively constituted, social representations (1954), the symbolic schemas themselves have been the focus of much exploration as have the strategies with which actors engage them (see Berger and Luckmann 1966; Bourdieu 1989; Hardin 1993). Scholars have used many rubrics to address these symbolic schemas: the moral imagination, the social imaginary, metaphor, and tropes are the most common, but all these approaches share various key features, such as a focus on representations and superstructure; an interest in the cultural processes that bind people together as they produce and reproduce social life; and an interest in the ways in which individuals and groups use symbolic, ideational material to improvise and organize action in social life.

Because social life includes the social imaginary,[11] we must focus on the representations that individuals and groups create, maintain, and reproduce. This interest in collective representations grows from Durkheim's sociological studies. In all their forms, these images—popular beliefs, cultural performances, and verbal arts—communicate cultural values and social relations (Bascom 1965), and people use them strategically in social life to accomplish their goals (Bauman 1977). "It is these representations, these beautiful stories that we tell ourselves, that structure individual and collective development. We might say, in a metaphorical way, that they serve as a counterpoint, as an accompanying music to the sinuous flow of human existence" (Maffesoli 1993c:64). Because individuals use the social imaginary to picture the world and work upon it, it provides "a means by which people extend their vision of what is possible" (Beidelman 1986:1).

The imaginary, especially as produced in representations, provides people with the opportunity to reflect upon and evaluate their worlds; here its complementarity with performance studies becomes most evident. The social imaginary is constituted of representations, and those representations are manifested in social life *by means of performance* (cf. Bauman 1989:262–263; Schechner and Appel 1990). Once performed, these images become part of the fabric of life. They play a key role in the social construction of reality, and people use them to structure their experiences and their subsequent performances. These performances taken in unison make up what Mauss (1973:73) and Bourdieu (1989:72) call *habitus,* that collection of bodily actions and transferable dispositions that form the lifeworld of each individual. In social life, individuals reproduce these images and the habitus of which they are constitutive, and they do so in particular arrangements that correspond to the structural properties guiding action at that time; in turn, their actions affect the structural properties themselves (Hardin 1993:15–21, 272). When considered more statically, representations allow scholars to explore cultural ideals, and when considered in practice and social use, they give scholars entry into the process of social production and reproduction.

This process must be understood as an attempt to bind people together. For Durkheim this social binding is the primary and quintessential function of all social representations, and the totem was a representation of society standing for an individual's relationship to the group (1954). For his modern French students all representations have this same, basically religious function. Michel Maffesoli has written extensively on the prevalence of representations as binding agents (see Maffesoli 1988). He argues that the image can be material, immaterial, or even simply an idea that people communicate about, but whatever the case "the central point or essential function which one can ascribe . . . to the image is that it leads to 'binding' (*reliance*), to what Durkheim calls the 'social divine'" (Maffesoli 1993a:4). These representations bind people together precisely because they allow them to operate within the same cosmology or world view, what Maffesoli (1993b) calls the "social ambiance."

This social ambiance must be maintained through social and cultural practices enacted by individuals. These socially given images allow individuals to use them in ever changing and flexible ways. Certainly these images reveal a great deal about the lived experience of the people who use them (Fernandez 1986; Jackson 1989:137–155; Lienhardt 1961:147–170), but they are also the symbolic resources employed to deal with new problems.[12] As cultural resources deployed at critical moments, socially given images provide an access point to explore individuals' behaviors and conceptions of that behavior; in much the same way, images provide people with standards and thus the means to evaluate and comment on the behavior of their peers.

The themes that appear repeatedly in different representations direct us to the key symbolic issues within a given culture, and people employ, improvise upon, and transform the images that express those themes. To explore the social imaginary, many different representations must be compared—ideally, the most highly marked cultural performances contrasted with the most quotidian practices and socially controlled discourse with the idle chatter of the most average people.[13] Common motifs reveal the essential themes, and the social and the cultural must be articulated fully. As Clifford Geertz has written:

> The application of critical categories to social events and sociological categories to symbolic structures is not some primitive form of philosophical mistake, nor is it another mere confusion of art and life. It is the proper method for a study dedicated to getting straight how the massive fact of cultural and historical particularity comports with the equally massive fact of cross-cultural and cross-historical accessibility—how the deeply different can be deeply known with becoming any less different; the enormously distant enormously close without becoming any less far away. (1983:48)

Although Geertz addresses himself to the problem of cross-cultural translation, he does provide a method for the study of the moral imagination, a method similar to the ones used by Beidelman (1986), Comaroff (1985), Fernandez (1982), and Jackson (1986).

PRINCIPLES OF ACTION

I am having another long phone conversation with Ernesto Pichardo,[14] the famous italero[15] from Miami. He has been answering my questions and teaching me divination since I was initiated as a priest in July 1992. He was initiated in 1971 as a young man and immediately began training as a diviner and master of ceremonies (Lu. *italero, oríaté*). His practical experience is beyond question. He has an incisive and analytical mind with which he has reflected on the social and ritual workings of the religion. I have learned a great deal from him.

It is the evening of October 23, 1995. I sit at my desk in Washington, D.C., as Pichardo elaborates his notions of aché. As I scribble notes, the conversation moves between English and Spanish[16]:

Ashé is the mana of every person and every object. The capacities of human beings to attract the spirits and divinities are one aspect of it, and each object has its own ashé. When you bring it into relation with another object, it becomes a new ashé. The introduction of the object forms a new mixture and the energy changes the situation. It transforms and becomes demonstrable and visible. If a situation requires aspirin and that is all that is required to change the situation, the aspirin has shown its ashé. Thus the object's ashé depends on the context in which it is being used.

People are different. If your know-how is extensive, then the work of the orishas is extensive. If not, then the work of the orichas will only reflect your human capacity. The ability of the communicator is key. It's just like in the Christian church. The institution is limited by the ability of the people in that institution. Because of the knowledge that an individual may have, it is that natural ability plus the learned that will make the difference between one priest and another. Natural ability and learning must go together, because ability cannot be relied on 100 percent, unless you are going to rely on possession 100 percent of the time. Even then, you have to know how to draw in possession and that is learned.

The ashé of an individual is more flexible than the ashé of an object because of our capacities and our characters. Character, the level of spiritual development, and the initiations a person has undergone all affect the ashé of an individual person. When a person makes orisha [is initiated as a priest or priestess], the ashé goes inside and outside. The ceremony introduces the divinity's energy into this specific body. Over time, that ashé is discharged and recharged because of different ceremonies that are done by the individual. With an aleyo there is nothing in the body and the ashé is not maintained in the same manner. Even after initiation, you still have to transform the human, and the divinity's energy transforms with that body. When the orisha first comes down and possesses a priest, it is mute. Later, after ashé is given to the mouth, it is vocalized and can speak. You will see that first it speaks very clearly in Yoruba, then in a mix of Yoruba and Spanish, and then more and more in Spanish or whatever the native language of the priest is. But it never loses the Yoruba, and the orisha's body language always responds to the content of the Yoruba chants.

After a person has that supernatural presence with the orisha, the individual must function as a receptor and radiator of that energy. The person's ability to

move that supernatural presence and to attract other energies makes the difference between one person's ashé and another.[17]

Within the Regla de Ocha, practitioners identify two interrelated series of
principles upon which they structure their actions. Just as these principles
come into play in the social field through action, they are also discussed
and debated within the discursive practices of the tradition. The first set
of principles is discussed in the generalities of belief among practitioners
and is manifest in practically all cultural performances. The second set of
principles grows from the first and is specific to individuals; these principles arise from particular divination rituals performed when orichas are
"born." Taken together these two groups of principles constitute an essential part of the habitus of the tradition.

1. Orichas and egun are living beings that affect human life. The fact
that practitioners describe orichas as being "born" in ritual underscores
the vitality the divinities have for their followers. Similarly the spirits are
said to "eat," "speak," "work," and "mount"; this discourse reveals the
agency attributed to these spirits. Their effects on the world are described
in many ways. Cosmogonically, before birth each individual is believed to
agree with an oricha to serve that power while on earth. This "head"
oricha protects and guides the individual and is ultimately responsible for
her success on earth. Individual character and comportment do determine
the quality of the relationship between the "head" oricha and the individual, and a successful person has the blessings of the orichas, blessings that
can be seen in the traditional prayers for "health, luck, tranquility, resolve, strength, and spiritual evolution."[18]

Each oricha is considered to "rule" a particular part of human life.
These correspondences between domains of human activity and specific
orichas are usually learned early in life by those born in the tradition and
quite soon by those entering the tradition as adults. Yemayá, the oricha of
the ocean, is also responsible for most aspects of motherhood. On the
most mundane level, she gives children to those who petition her, and she
protects children everywhere. She is also said to be the mother of all humans and "the first oricha to come to the defense of humanity."[19] In the
same way that Yemayá rules motherhood, Ochún is "the river and love
and all the good things in this life." Ochún rules the heart and gives
people the human love they need. She is the basic connection between
people that keeps society functioning, and in many of her stories she
solves a problem by making contact with another supernatural power.

Through their "rule" of different domains of human endeavor, the orichas affect the lives of their followers.

The effects that the spirits of the dead have on the living are both more frequent and less obvious. As a group, the dead are said to give people resolve. They are most often represented by a carved, figurative cane, and their presence is said to steady humans' lives. Spirits venerated include the deceased ancestors in the ritual family, those who have gone before in the blood family of the individual, and spirits who are otherwise essential because of some prenatal commitment to the individual (*cuadro espiritual*). Through dreams, intuitions, and revelations made at possession rituals given in their honor, the dead (Sp. *los muertos*) guide, protect, and heal the humans to whom they are connected. Within these general responsibilities, different categories of the dead are known for their skills in certain areas. The *congo* (Sp. of Bantu origin) spirits are thought to be strong-willed, powerful, and extremely good at guiding people through hostile social circumstances. The *gitano* (Sp. gypsy) spirits have terrific psychic powers and therefore warn people of impending troubles and diagnose and treat difficult illnesses. Similarly, known individual spirits continue to have the skills they possessed when alive. Thus, a person's wise mother might appear in a dream or a *misa* to offer moral guidance. Although these categorical skills are certainly based on stereotypes of social groups or on the attributes of deceased individuals, from a practical standpoint these spirits usually deliver as expected.

2. Every human being has an individual destiny in the world. Much of the traditional wisdom and cultural actions within the Regla de Ocha revolve around the nature of an individual's destiny. Called *destino* or *camino* (Sp. destiny, road), this aspect of life cannot be avoided by individuals. There is no widespread notion of absolute predetermination, but practitioners agree that certain issues and character traits repeatedly come into play in the life of specific individuals.

Elders in the tradition often say, "*Cada persona tiene su propio destino*" (each person has his/her own destiny) or "*cada cual vino al mundo con su propio camino*" (everyone came into the world with his/her own road). Practitioners employ the image of the road much more frequently than they refer to destiny itself, and the meanings of the roads are manifold. In a general sense, it refers to the future, and when it is used in this way, people will say there is an illness, obstacle, or blessing in your road. Another set of common expressions discusses the road as possibility and ease of movement. Practitioners will say that a person's roads are closed and prescribe particular ritual activities to open the road. Closed roads translate into the absence of opportunity and choice, a reduction in freedom. In fact, the trickster and messenger oricha Elegguá controls the road, and when positively predisposed to an individual "opens the road to blessings and closes the road to difficulties." Within the divination system known as the shells (Sp. *caracoles*) or *dilogún* (Lu. lit. sixteen, referring to the number of shells used), many proverbs associated with the 256 possible divination figures allude to destiny or the road. Here are a few examples from different divination figures[20]:

Ocana-Odí: "The one who does not take a known road gets lost and has to turn back" *(él que no va por camino conocido, pierde y tiene que virar hacia atrás)*. This proverb suggests that the individual follow a well-known course of action to avoid being set back. Another proverb is often quoted in this figure: "When the roads are closed, only intelligence, will, and faith open them" *(cuando los caminos se cierran, sólo la inteligencia los abre, con voluntad y fé, estos se abren)*. This proverb explains how one might open the roads when they are closed.

Ogunda-Odí: "If I keep my promise, my road will be straight" *(si cumplo lo que ofrezco mi camino será derecho)*. This proverb urges the individual to fulfill her duty in relation to the orichas and the spirits so that everything will turn out well.

Oché-Metanlá: "When a good road is chosen, the goal is reached" *(cuando se elige buen camino, se llega a la meta)*. Here the wisdom of the dilogún admonishes the individual to choose and follow a course of action carefully.

Obara-Odí: "The dog has four feet and takes a single road" *(el perro tiene cuatro patas y coge un solo camino)*. Practitioners regularly invoke the wisdom of this figure when they sense that an individual under their supervision has too many commitments or is attempting to keep too many options open at the same time.

These proverbs reveal the importance of the trope of the road. Although the details of a person's road can never be completely known, many ritual practices focus on discovering the nature of destiny.

3. Revelation, especially divination, reveals the essence of situations and problems as well as their solutions. As people work to understand their roads, they seek revelation from the dead and the orichas. In almost all cases the revelation has three components. It describes the person's circumstances in detail and thus establishes the credibility of the agent delivering the revelation. It articulates the origin of the situation; while at

times the source can be quite mundane, it is often quite extraordinary. Revelations also include prescriptions for solutions to any difficulties that may be present; these suggestions can address the behavior of the person, prescribe certain courses of action (like moving or not going on a planned trip), and list specific ritual work which the person needs to undertake to change the underlying, spiritual causes of the situation. Revelation establishes an interpretive frame for the situation, the specific circumstances in which the person finds herself, and a recommended course of action. Important revelations—like those made at initiations—often guide people as they make subsequent life decisions.

Revelation occurs primarily through one of three mechanisms: dreams, spirit possession, or divination. Dreams are the most unreliable but the most universally accessible. Although most people agree that the revelations of dreams must be authenticated by means of divination and there is disagreement about whether the dead or the orichas are responsible for dreams, their widespread presence makes dreams an extremely powerful and influential form of revelation. Through possession, spirits of the dead and the orichas appear to their followers in key ritual performances. Both usually spend time delivering messages to their followers, and people use this information to guide their choices and actions. During possession, very full revelation often transpires with the origin, specific circumstances, and the course of action all being articulated by a presence manifested from the otherworld. The dramatic texture of possession performances often makes these revelations particularly impressive to individuals who frequently recount them again and again when they are trying to explain their actions to people around them. However, some practitioners maintain that even these revelations must be verified through formal divination.

In the religion, three main forms of divination provide the mechanisms through which the spirits "speak." Coconut divination uses four pieces of coconut meat to answer yes-or-no questions. Rare are the initiates in the religion who do not know and use this system. People use it constantly to learn whether the spirits have accepted their sacrifices. People who have physical manifestations of the orichas living with them employ this system every week as they "attend" to their orichas. The shells are less widely available and less widely used. These sixteen opened cowrie shells are the "mouths of the oricha" and are tossed on a mat to reveal a specific odu. This figure refers to specific circumstances, relevant allegorical stories, applicable proverbs, praise songs, and advice. Priestesses and priests receive the shells when they are initiated and must study for years before they can understand and competently apply the 256 possible figures to the life of another person. Similarly, Ifá divination can only be learned by the men initiated into the priesthood (Sp. *culto*) of Orula. This divination system again has 256 possible outcomes but uses either sixteen palm nuts or an *ópele* (Lu.), a chain with eight concave disks, to identify the relevant divination figure. The dilogún and Ifá divination resemble each other in many ways, though some of the divination figures have different names.

Precisely because revelation plays such a critical role in the religion, different kinds of revelation are considered to have differing levels of accuracy. Although there is no universal agreement on this subject, perceived accuracy and reliability are related to the hierarchical position of the supernatural agent responsible for the revelation. Dreams, like revelations from reading cards or gazing into a crystal ball or glass of water, are often said to come from the dead. For most practitioners, the dead have less authority than do the orichas, so their revelations must be ratified by the orichas when there appears to be a contradiction between their wishes. Similarly, a priestess's head-ruling oricha has authority over all of the other orichas, so for example, no priestess of Ochún would follow advice from Ogún that contradicted advice already received from Ochún. Over all of these powers Orula's revelations have final authority. When there is any serious dispute between divinities over the life of a person, that individual seeks the guidance of Ifá divination, because Orula alone has the authority to negotiate claims between different orichas.

4. The correct ebó performed at the right time in the proper way beneficially changes the objective circumstances of the person who offers it. The word *ebó* cannot be translated easily, although it is a core religious concept in the Regla de Ocha. The root *bo* means "to adore" or "to worship," and the prefix indicates that the verb has been transformed into a noun; thus *ebó* indicates an act of worship or adoration of the spirits. These acts of adoration take a wide number of forms: They include prayers (Lu. *adurá*), the use of medicines to affect the body (Lu. *ogún*), observing taboos set by the spirits (Lu. *ewó*), small food offerings (Lu. *adimú*), spiritual baths and cleansings (Lu. *ebó kere*), offerings to the head (Lu. *eborí eledá*), blood sacrifice (Lu. *ebó eyé* or *ebó oto eye balé*), and the drumming rituals where the orichas "come down."[21] The various initiations within the religion also serve as ebó, whether the early ceremony of placing the necklaces upon a new godchild, the receiving of an oricha to attend to and interact with, or the dedication of a whole person's life to the orichas in the asiento, the initiation of a new priest.

Regardless of the form it takes, ebó always relates humans to the spiritual world. In the cosmology of the Regla de Ocha, all of existence resides in one of two realms: *Ayé* represents the phenomenal and visible world, the land of the living, and the theater of human endeavor, and *orun* (Lu. heaven, the otherworld) contains the powerful and potentially dangerous agency of the spirits.[22] Ebó serves to bridge these realms and to facilitate communication between them. Considered schematically, the religion's practices can be grouped into divination, sacrifice, and possession. In divination humans seek information from the spiritual world; in sacrifice, humans offer food to the powers of the otherworld; and in possession, these worlds fuse briefly for the benefit of both.[23] In fact, most ritual performances include some mixture of these idealized categories; for example, a dilogún divination ritual opens with an invocation of the dead and the orichas and an offering of water and money to the oricha who will speak. Such a ritual reveals the impact of the otherworld on this world and prescribes a specific type of ebó.

For any specific ebó to be efficacious, it must contain the correct ingredients and be performed in the proper way. Practitioners have certain cultured expectations about which *eboces*[24] for which orichas assist humans with which kinds of problems, but these generalizations do not always apply. Ochún is famous for helping barren women become pregnant after she receives an ebó of a pumpkin filled with honey, cinnamon, cloves, and vanilla—all foods that she favors. Practitioners know this ebó to be powerful and often employed, though it does not always produce the desired effect. When an ebó does not work, practitioners will choose one of three explanations. They might suggest that the priestess who made the ebó does not have aché in a general sense, that she lacks the basic generative power to effect changes in the spiritual and phenomenal worlds. They might also suggest that the ebó was done incorrectly. Although the priestess has aché and this ebó was the appropriate one for the circumstances, some flaw in the ritual performance impeded its effectiveness. The possible flaws are virtually infinite, but in each case an oversight or a mistake in the ritual process has rendered the ebó ineffective. Third, practitioners might suggest that the ebó performed was not the correct one for the situation. Here again explanations abound. In addition to Ochún, Yemayá also assists those seeking children and perhaps a similar ebó should have been offered to her. Perhaps a malicious spirit has been sent against the mother-to-be and is interfering with the conception process. Though many speculations emerge from failed eboces, the religious ideology says that accurate divination reveals the correct ebó, including its timing, its ingredients, and their number. A specific ebó performed correctly by a competent priestess should change the dynamics in the spiritual world and thereby transform the situation in the physical world.

5. Respect must be paid to the elders and, by extension, to tradition. This principle of the religious ideology of the Regla de Ocha structures much of social life and symbolic action. Upon initiation as a priest, ritual kin relationships come into play with the neophyte as godchild and the initiator as godparent. A godchild always owes respect to her godparents, and for many people this rule is incontrovertible and absolute. Frequently this ideal results in godchildren reproducing the performances of their godparents in a rigid and unreflective way. Justifications of ritual actions often include appeals such as "My godfather did it that way and so do I" and "It is done in that way in my branch of the religion." This emulation of the godparent as a carrier of the tradition works to reproduce and "traditionalize" social and cultural forms in an extremely precise way, although other practitioners may offer critiques of these performances. Of course, social life includes a good dose of acrimony, and godchildren and godparents struggle with one another and at times separate permanently.[25]

Even in the most extreme situations, however, godchildren are expected to name their godparents when they pay tribute to all the spirits and humans with whom they work in the religion. The *moyuba,* an important verbal form in the tradition, is a long invocation that lists and honors all the egun, orichas, and priests and priestesses with whom a practitioner has had a relationship, and the prayer ends with invocations of protection for living godparents and others who have initiated the speaker, regardless of their current social relationship. Other verbal forms reveal the importance of this respect. Proverbs on the subject are manifold. "The ears do not pass the head" (Sp. *las orejas no pasan la cabeza*) points to the proper relationship of minors to elders with the minors below. The elders should lead the minors in all things. People commonly say "Respect to be respected" (Sp. *respete para que lo respeten*) to explain a moral course of action. Respectful people often garner the respect of others, but it is in no way guaranteed.

A key ideological proverb says, "The dead gave birth to the orichas" (Sp. *los muertos parieron a los orichas,* Lu. *egun lobi ocha*). This statement encodes both a prescription for ritual action and a profound truth about the history of the tradition. The widely held belief is that practitioners must "work" the dead before they work the orichas to show respect to the dead and to have an open road with the orichas. In ritual, the dead are named and consulted before the orichas, and this proverb is the common explanation. The proverb also leads practitioners to reflect on the fact that they have received the orichas through a lineage of ritual ancestors, and in their initiation, their orichas were "born" from their godparents' manifestations of the divinities. Because the orichas have come through the elders, living and dead, the elders deserve respect on a never-ending basis.

In addition to respect for the dead, this proverb also underscores the importance of traditionalization as a key practice within the religion. By linking present or proposed practices, values, meanings, and expressive forms to symbolic material from the past, Santería practitioners can traditionalize their actions (see Handler and Linnekin 1984; Hobsbawm and Ranger 1983). Tradition, then, is understood as a specific, context-derived interpretation and representation of the *present* in terms of its connections—real or imagined—with the *past* (Hymes 1975; Bauman 1992). Traditionalization in Santería provides practitioners with an explanation for the source of their practices as well as moral authority to enact those practices.

Just as verbal forms demonstrate respect and traditionalization, ritual minors must do moforibale to their elders in ritual and social contexts. This prostration embodies the relationship of respect that plays such a key role in the tradition. This bodily ritual form demonstrates the social deference that minors ideally show their elders. Through the ritual kin system, through verbal forms, and through the use of the body, followers of the orichas again and again show the importance of respecting the elders.

But ritual age and respect for elders as structuring principles are crosscut by the importance given to ritual position within a given performance context. Ritual age is the dominant form of hierarchy within the religion, but this social structure competes with certain ritual functions at ceremonies. Just as revelations possess differing validity depending on the source of the oracular statement, certain social roles are more important than others in a given context, and the social order usually adjusts accordingly. The best and most common example is the italero or oríaté who enters important ritual ceremonies, and, though usually an elder, must command the assembled priestesses and priests regardless of their relative positions in the age-based hierarchy. For the duration of the ceremony, the ritual specialist sits atop the hierarchy.

In addition to these five generalized principles and growing from the importance of divination, revelations given to each individual priest and priestess at the time of their initiations undergird the habitus of the Regla de Ocha. These principles are both cultured and individual. Many of the practices enacted by individuals relate directly to the divination ritual called the *itá* that provides each actor with a specific and fairly limited set of divination verses with which to understand life and engage the world. These verses reveal basic issues of character, sociability, health, and economics that will confront the individual again and again. They also contain stories and proverbs considered key to the person's destiny. Because of their relationship to destiny and their great value, many practitioners refuse to reveal the contents of their itá to anyone. Most practitioners believe that individuals act out these stories and proverbs for better or worse and so are challenged to manifest them positively. In general, people ensure these positive manifestations by making ebó of some sort.

From the tropes of this allegorical material, practitioners improvise individualized action to maximize their circumstances. Cognitively oriented anthropologists have long been interested in the effects of metaphors and other linguistic tropes on cultural life (Fernandez 1991; Lakoff and Johnson 1980), and much has been made of the ability of metaphor to unite disparate realms of experience (Jackson 1989:137–155). In this analogical mode of thought and action, the source image (the item which is symbolically brought into play) is transferred and mapped onto the target situation (the situation or object symbolically described by the source). In the case of oricha divination the source can be in a story or a proverb, and the target is or will be present in the life of the practitioner. Because the source of the metaphoric situation will manifest again and again but in unpredictable ways, practitioners attempt to identify ways to make their actions embody the source and thereby become the target of the tropes. Through this elaborate, symbolic work, priestesses and priests of the orichas attempt to accomplish their goals at the same time that their lives literally embody some manifestation of the divination sign that the orichas have determined to be relevant.

The divination figures contain "secrets" that identify the person with the allegorical material elicited from the itá divination ceremony. These secrets can take the form of repeated stereotyped behavior or some object that embodies certain aspects of the divination sign. For example, the divination sign Iroso Meyi advises the person to make ebó every month; this course of action responds to the character of the odu in which nothing is accomplished without hard and consistent labor. Similarly the sign Obara-Eyeunle includes a story about a town that had to make ebó two days in a row and this same course of action is suggested for the person who "has" this odu.[26] The odu Oché-Iroso includes the proverb, "If the water does not fall, the corn will not grow," and as a rule children of this figure wear a necklace of roasted corn to identify themselves with the idealized, productive result in the source proverb. These relatively simple examples provide a taste of the open "secrets" of the odus, which result in symbolic actions by practitioners.

Beyond these more generally applied and cultured patterns of action, practitioners also improvise actions based on the odus. A brief example of this kind of symbolic action will provide some sense of divination's effects on further cultural performances. The divination figure called Oché-Odí includes the following proverbs: "The one who owes and pays his debt is free" and "It is not good to say everything nor is it good to eat everything." The figure also includes a long story describing how the red parrot feather came to protect people from witchcraft. This figure came out for a santero with whom I work here in Washington, D.C., when we were preparing to go to a ritual drumming in New York. As we prepared for the trip, he followed the tropes from the figure: He made an outstanding sacrifice to the orichas, thus paying what he owed. He wore a protective red parrot feather hidden under his cap at the drumming, thus integrating the warning about witchcraft from the story and the idea of secrecy from the proverb, "It is not good to say everything nor is it good to eat everything." This brief example illustrates how santeros use these traditional expressive forms to improvise symbolic actions.

In fact, the divination signs' stories and proverbs act as generative schemata for practitioners. They mobilize and deploy the verbal texts from their personal divination signs with the goal of incarnating them; this transference of the sign into lived experience and social action is key to these more individual cultural principles. As Bourdieu has said, "Practical logic . . . is able to organize the totality of an agent's thoughts, perceptions, and actions by means of a few generative principles. . . . These discrete, self-sufficient units owe their immediate transparency not only to the schemes which are realized in them, but also to the *situation* apprehended through these schemes and to the agent's practical relationship to the situation" (1989:110). The schemes present in the texts manifest as the actions of intentional actors in the social field that includes the gods as primary agents. Thus practitioners follow the advice of the orichas by improvising or embodying the actions related to the odu. Through the use of these tropes, practitioners unite the ideal and eternal orun with the everyday reality of action in the tangible and observable ayé.[27]

VYING FOR POWER: EVALUATION, STATUS, AND ACHÉ

This uniting of worlds never happens in isolation, however. As a priest attempts to enact the allegorical patterns of his itá, he is constantly being watched and judged by his peers. The general principles I articulated before and those symbolic resources relevant to the divination figures from the itá represent the key patterned, yet idiosyncratic, idioms of experience in the Regla de Ocha. These idioms are manifestations of what Anthony Giddens (1979) has called structural properties—properties that shape traditions, values, cultural notions of personhood, and behavior. Evaluation focuses on certain kinds of action, and it gathers around the ways in which people deploy these structural properties.

These evaluations establish certain aspects of status, and criticism must be understood as a key cultural form that results in differential access to power in certain situations (Hardin 1993:189–264). Though not called "ceremonies" by practitioners, these verbal contestations and defenses of social power must be understood as a less clearly marked but still very important form of ritual. Competence as a religious performer results in a certain level of status, but each performance potentially evokes evaluation and criticism that revise the status granted to performers; this potential for criticism often leads practitioners to a reflexive position in which they anticipate critiques and prepare explanations and justifications. The semiotic communication embedded in each performance contextualizes that event within an evaluative frame (Bauman and Briggs 1990); within the Regla de Ocha, the frame itself often becomes the ground of contestation as practitioners seek status and power.

Status competition plays a critical role within the religion precisely because of the hierarchical nature of the semisecret society of oricha practitioners. There is a widely accepted hierarchy of fully initiated priests and priestesses in the religion; this idealized hierarchy is reproduced in discourse and practice again and again. The babalawo holds a great deal of power in some circles because of his access to Ifá divination. As noted earlier, his divinations are widely considered to be the most accurate; ideology states that all other opinions must be subsumed under his authority, although in practice practitioners can subvert his authority in any number of ways. Babalawos with Olofi are rarer, even in Cuba (cf. Sánchez 1978:30); these babalawos have the authority and ritual capacity to initiate others into Ifá. Babalawos with *kuanaldo* (Lu.), an initiation that allows a babalawo to slaughter four-legged animals, are fairly common (Brandon 1983:

392 and 396; Murphy 1988:85–87); even in small communities, like Washington, D.C., there are babalawos with kuanaldo. *Oluos* (Lu. lords) are those babalawos who made oricha before making Ifá and thus have some authority in both domains, although they cannot initiate people to orichas other than Orula.

The oríaté and the italero are both common and frequently have large followings of divination clients who visit them regularly. At this level, status competition leads people to criticize each other's practice, knowledge, and preparation and ultimately to question the authority and competence of their competitors. Under the italeros are those practitioners who "have ocha"; the terms *oloricha* and *olocha* (Lu. owner of oricha) reflect this connective relationship. Those olochas with *cuchillo* (Sp. knife) or *pinaldo* (Lu. knife), an initiation that is commonly interpreted to authorize them to sacrifice four-legged animals, have more status than others. *Iyalochas* and *babalochas* (Lu. mother- and father-of-oricha) are those priestesses and priests who have initiated another person into the priesthood. Positions within this idealized hierarchy are always being contested and revised, and evaluation and criticism function as omnipresent tools in the struggle for respect and status.[28]

This ideologically driven hierarchy derives primarily from generalized and objective notions of personhood. These notions of personhood, however, must be appropriated by living individuals if they are to embody and experience the qualities and capacities associated with their cultural notions (Fortes 1973:287). The five general principles of action adumbrated earlier correspond roughly with these generalized notions of personhood and the status granted through initiations while, at the same time, those individualized principles of action generated from the itá correspond with the subjective and lived experience of personhood. Criticism focuses both on the performance and its implications for the moral person responsible for that performance. Positive evaluations of a given ritual performance imply that the person has aché; it is common to hear practitioners say, "She is a tremendous priestess" (Sp. *es tremenda santera*). Similarly, a practitioner's criticism of a ritual performance is tantamount to a critique of the person's ability as a practitioner and morality as a member of the community. In the final analysis, the general principles of action are the ones applied to practitioners when they are evaluated by their peers. Performative competence and moral personhood become roughly equivalent.

For example, every olocha should be able to recite the long Lucumí invocation called the moyuba that opens every ceremony. This prayer represents a key performance that is repeated with great frequency, and elders expect everyone to have mastered it relatively early in their lives as olochas. In reality, of course, some people fail to learn the prayer, and that failure can evoke extremely harsh criticism. In a ritual context, elders might rebuke or belittle those who do not know this basic ritual element. An individual might be expert at transforming the allegories of divination figures into elegant symbolic actions, though peers will never perceive those actions for what they are and so must judge on the more generalized forms of action within the tradition.

Naturally, the situation exacerbates the difficulties inherent in the secrecy of the itá. Because people act on the secret content of their itá, their actions are beyond the evaluation of most other people. At the same time, however, their joint membership in a secret priesthood unites them symbolically and leads to heightened social awareness (Herdt 1990:371–372). This awareness leads directly to self-evaluation, and the secret symbolic actions are performances with extremely limited audiences usually consisting of the person's godparents and the spirits. Though a person may very well act from a personal interpretation of an odu, it is fairly uncommon to communicate the odus from the itá to outsiders. Thus one practitioner may improvise actions based on a sign only to be evaluated on the more general aspects of performance. An actor may have one secret explanation for her actions and be criticized for—and defend—the same actions using the more common understandings of appropriate ritual actions. Here the competence of the performance can depend on which frame is used to understand and evaluate it. Thus the deployment of these schemes is always political and contested.

Within the religion's multiplicity, it is possible to observe and articulate two notions that lie at opposite ends of a continuum used in evaluating people and their ritual performances. At one end of this continuum lies the idea of a *good heart* (Sp. *buen corazón*) and at the other the idea of *understanding* (Sp. *conocimiento, entendimiento*). Priestesses tend to evaluate others more in terms of the quality of the heart, whereas priests of various categories tend to evaluate others more in terms of their understanding. Certainly these evaluative categories are not mutually exclusive, as is clear from the explanation of aché given by Luisa, but they are frequently used by different segments of the religious population.

To have a good heart reflects a subjective interest in dispositions, attitudes, desires, feeling, sentiment, and affect. The general moral character and the current moral status of the person determine whether a person has a good heart. When asked, practitioners most frequently describe a good heart as "clean" and "disinterested" (Sp. *limpio; sin interés*). A clean heart harbors neither envy nor betrayal, two negative emotions that are understood to have independent agency within the religion. A Washington priestess of Yemayá said to me, "I want people to know the orichas and the egun and to know that this is a clean religion" (Bravos Pineda 1993). The notion of acting with or without interest has currency in the larger Cuban and Cuban-American cultural milieu. To be disinterested is not to be indifferent, but rather to have no ulterior motives in a given situation.[29]

Although these explanations are negatively defined, a good heart can also be defined positively. A person who has a good heart acts with generosity toward others and stresses the bonds of reciprocity that link people to each other and to the spirits. When these notions structure actions, they result in the creation and maintenance of social relationships over long periods of time, relationships that come to be characterized by expressions of deep loyalty. A priestess in Havana once introduced me to another priestess, saying, "She has a good heart, and she is like a member of my family." As she spoke, tears appeared in her eyes. "She is of the house and we trust in her." This simple example epitomizes the emotional and relational aspects of a good heart.

Contrasted with the good heart is the pursuit of conocimiento. Because of the secrecy of the tradition, esoteric knowledge frequently translates into social power. To have understanding is to be able to explain the origin of a practice and the origin of a specific understanding of that practice. Within the religion, origins play a key role in justifying knowledge and actions. Practitioners of the Regla de Ocha engage in a practice they call "*recopilación*" (Sp. compilation) in which they gather together all the information they can about religious practices that are important to them. This information includes Lucumí words and phrases, melodies and lyrics of praise songs, ritual genealogies, specific sacrifices appropriate for certain circumstances, divination stories and proverbs, herbal knowledge, and how and when to conduct certain ceremonies. Because the itá reveals certain important areas of endeavor for each individual, the areas researched usually relate to the itá, and that research leads practitioners to a wide variety of activities including consulting wise and respected elders; studying ethnographic texts about Yoruba, Cuban, and Brazilian variants of the religion; and acquiring and learning from texts produced by respected elders.

Of these different activities, consulting respected elders continues to play the most important role in recopilación. People call their elders in other cities and in Cuba with great regularity, and practitioners will travel to visit elders who have a great deal to offer. In recent years, practitioners in the United States—African Americans, Cuban Americans, Euro-Americans, and Latin Americans—have traveled to Cuba to gather information about the tradition through initiation and consultation with elders on the island. Similarly, increasing numbers of people have traveled to Nigeria to seek the "roots" of the religion in Africa (see Brandon 1993; D. Brown 1995). However, recopilación frequently results in social tensions. Because the source of knowledge is of such importance to its value, knowledge from an unknown elder may result in efficacious religious ritual but be of little enduring social value.

Displays of understanding always include some explanation of the social source of that understanding. People frequently say, "The little understanding I have comes from my godfather." The implication is that the knowledge is therefore sound and reliable, and to question that intellectual formulation is to socially attack the person and his or her ritual lineage. When an explanation is put forth, it may make sense but the person who put it forth may be questionable, and therefore it draws criticism. To display understanding of a certain ritual requires verbal performative competence and an understanding of the evaluative criteria used by the other people present. Here verbal displays of understanding link ritual performances and social status. Again performance knowledge and individual morality influence one another.

Because consulting elders plays such an important role in gaining and defending understanding, this pole of the evaluative continuum also encourages certain kinds of sociability. Although understanding must be guarded and protected from others if a person is to maintain status, its generation requires people to work with their elders. Only through respectful social relationships does understanding move from one person to another. Although a focus on understanding usually results in more competitive behavior than would a focus on a good heart, these two evaluative notions inform much of the criticism by which people vie for social power and performative authority in the Regla de Ocha.

When I became a priest and the orichas spoke to me, they gave me the name Ocán Oñí (Lu. Heart of Honey). Only as I reflected on this chapter did the irony of this name strike me. My oricha name clearly links me to the "good heart" end of the ritual continuum. In contrast, my divination teacher,

Ernesto Pichardo, has dedicated himself to enumerating the principles involved in the ceremonies that give life and presence to the orichas. He constantly pushes me to think in terms of "understanding." His instruction is one of the many blessings I have received from the orichas, and his loyalty and patience have provided me with whatever understanding and reputation I have in the religion. Under his guidance I consecrated a priestess of the orichas in April 1996 and went on to consecrate three more in 1998.

Through ritual lineage connections with Pichardo in Miami and my godmother and her family in Havana, I have learned the basic workings of the religion both as a practice and a theological system of thought. This intimate knowledge of the religion has placed me in extended social relationships with those people that some anthropologists might refer to and think of as "informants."[30] My ongoing relationships with these and other people force me consistently to engage in participatory experiences that extend my embodied knowledge of Santería as both an affective force in their lives and mine and an extraordinarily complex system of knowledge (see Okely 1992).

The same year that I became interested in Santería, I began to study folklore and anthropology. In 1989 I began my graduate work in folklore at Indiana University. I chose folklore in part because the writing of so many anthropologists avoided the human component of culture; frequently discussions of social life did not include people but only aggregates and structures. Within folkloristics I have struggled to integrate the analytics of practice theory and performance studies with the phenomenological descriptions of the anthropology of experience. I have sought to explain how religious practitioners create their gods and then cope with their demands as these practitioners understand and work upon their lifeworlds. Richard Bauman, Michael Jackson, and Robert Orsi have generously given their time helping to inspire and birth these ideas. Their varied lineage connections are clear in my approach, my citations, and my style. Through them I have learned folklore and cultural anthropology as professional and cultural practices and as an exploratory system of thought.

As a santero and an anthropological folklorist, I must continue to perform within the generic conventions established by those discourses. Although these discourses have traditionally suggested different positions and intellectual assumptions, my subjectivity—both socially and personally—cannot be separated from these discourses, and in each I have struggled to balance the cognitive and the affective, the analytic and the empathetic. Moreover, my academic endeavors cannot be separated from my regular

work as a priest. The social constitution of human and supernatural subjectivity undergirds this work and informs each ceremony I perform.
Undergoing rituals like the asiento and graduate school and taking titles
like "olocha" and "doctor" changed this subject's state and knowledge,
but only by means of performance is that state fully inhabited and sustained and that knowledge realized in action. Only ceremonies and professional activities sustain the subjects thus created.

Rather than consider reified traditions that have come together to create
the complex of cultural practices known as Santería or the Regla de Ocha,
this chapter has explored the agency of those people who practice this religious tradition. Beginning with ideas about aché, the generative power
that allows people to accomplish things in the social and supernatural
worlds, it argues against a focus on syncretism as an especially valuable
subcategory of cultural change. Instead, it articulates the imagination of
powerful actions by people inside the religion in an attempt to explore the
lifeworld they inhabit. By examining how people imagine power and action, it is possible to sketch out two related sets of principles of action, one
general and the other based on the results of key divination rituals. These
principles come into play as the social and cultural practices of the followers of the religion, and they employ these same principles as they evaluate
and criticize each other. Ultimately the skill and creativity with which
people use these principles and these critiques determine the extent of their
social power in any given context. Performative competence produces social power, and aché lies somewhere between a ritual performer's natural
abilities and learned behaviors. Aché must be claimed and defended in
real-life situations if it is to be generative in any meaningful way, as the following vignette illustrates.

It is July 3, 1992. After my initiation, just after the completion of the itá
on the third day, the italero and Eugenia—a senior priestess of Ochún
and my godmother's aunt—have a loud argument. She says, "In all my
thirty-two years in this religion, I have never been in a house for an itá
and not received a derecho."

The italero retorts, "You were not in the room and so you did not receive a derecho," as he moves toward her.

"It is a lack of respect that allows you to do this to me. I have never seen
such behavior before," she says looking away but staying put. "I was
washing orichas before you were born [in the religion]."

"Perhaps you were, but I am the one they hired to make this oricha and I am the one who is responsible for what goes on here. You were not in the room and so you do not receive a derecho."

"I am the oldest priestess here and you, you are going to deny me a derecho? Be careful. Be careful. Ochún does not tolerate this kind of behavior. Be careful that you don't make a big mistake," she comes back even louder than before.

My godmother pipes in. She is Eugenia's sister in the religion as well as her niece. "You cannot do this here, not now, not here. We have just made an oricha, and you cannot have an argument like this here, not now." Eugenia now turns her back to the italero, a gesture of disrespect and anger, and says to her niece, "I am your elder and I am his elder and in all my years in this religion I have never seen this kind of thing. When Benigna— Ochún Toquín—was alive, she would never do this kind of thing. When she made Lourdes's oricha, I worked in the kitchen, but Berta—Ochún Funqué—your mother came into that kitchen and handed me the derecho. Someone has to do that work and it's a lot harder than sitting on your ass in the room. Ochún Toquín would never have allowed this."

The godmother responds, "Calm down, quiet down, you know we cannot have an argument here."

The italero moves in front of Eugenia and says as politely as he can in his frustration, "Look, your godmother may have given you a derecho when you were in the kitchen in Cárdenas, but I am not going to give you one here in Havana. I am sorry, señora, but that is not going to happen here today. My godfather—Kuko who lived across from your house in Old Havana—taught me that only the people in the room get derechos."

Eugenia is quieting down now. "The head carries the body," she says ironically but submissively. "The head carries the body, but you are no Kuko." The fight is over. The italero has gotten his way, but not without a final insult from Eugenia.

6

SANTERÍA AND THE SOCIAL
CONSTRUCTION OF SUBJECTIVITY

After first reading a description of Santería in 1986, I was fascinated by the richly detailed stories about the orichas—the gods with whom all practitioners regularly have intimate interactions. At that time I was particularly drawn to the oricha Oyá, the tumultuous goddess who rules the spirits of the dead and sends violent storms to transform human lives. The day I read about her, I dreamed that I was calling her name and she responded to me.

From the beginning, my research on the religion has been fueled by both intellectual curiosity and spiritual fervor, and through the years I have repeatedly opened myself to the passion and power of the orichas— through dreams, participant observation in religious ceremonies performed for others, and undergoing various initiations committing me to the service of Ochún, the sweet oricha of the river. Children of Ochún are famous for their ability to divine through dreams, and this portal to the invisible world of orun opens to me from time to time. Recently, Ochún sent the following dream:

I am attending a seminar in a room with large glass windows all around that look out over the Malecón, the seawall avenue that runs along the northern shore of Havana. We are discussing oricha theology and directions that still need to be explored. After listening to scholars and religious elders speak their minds, I begin to speak in Spanish, "What we have failed to account for is the dynamic relationship between the oricha and practitioner. They are in a relationship with each other, and yet they are both changing all the time. We think of the orichas as eternal and unchanging. They are eternal, but unchanging? No. Look outside, look at the sea today. Yemayá [oricha of the ocean] does not look like she did yesterday. She does not look the same in the east where it is stormy as she does in the west where it is sunny." In the stormy eastern sky, I see the figure of Yemayá dancing.

As a practitioner of the religion, I must see this dream as a revelation from the orichas, a distillation of a message they have sent me. As a scholar, it contains the kernel of an idea I have pursued in this text: It is in the changing relationships that human beings forge with the orichas that we can best explore and understand the Regla de Ocha.

RITUAL PERFORMANCE AND SUBJECTIVITY IN SANTERÍA

Ritual performances, usually called *ceremonias* (Sp. ceremonies), represent a central cultural domain for Santería practitioners who perform and participate in them to make sense of their experiences and to work upon their lifeworlds; thus, religious ritual represents one tool with which Santería practitioners can address the circumstances in which they find themselves. Ritual is thought to change situations in the "real world," and as an initiatory religion, the Regla de Ocha transforms human subjectivity by placing it into increasingly intimate relations with the subjectivity of the supernaturals.[1] Through the instrumentality of ritual, practitioners evoke different social positions that culturally imply differing capacities, competencies, and authority. Participating as the intended beneficiary of a ritual transforms an individual's subjectivity in important ways, at the same time that performing a ritual reinforces a priestess's subjectivity and her role as an "instrument of the orichas." The person for whom a ceremony is performed usually experiences a sense of increased possibility after the rituals because of the new knowledge and new capacities that typically accompany these performances. In turn, new understanding and capabilities often result in additional ritual performances by that same person.

In a consulta with the cowrie shells, the diviner consults an oricha, mediates between the client and the orichas to explore different domains of the client's life, and usually addresses the client's character, social circumstances, health, and financial situation. As different aspects of identity emerge in the conversation, the diviner locates the source of the client's misfortune, whether it is natural or supernatural. The diviner then identifies which religious acts dedicated to which supernatural subjects will ameliorate the client's situation. If the client follows through and makes the ebó, she must submit herself to the supernatural subject who has come forth "to defend" her. Thus, the understanding that emerges in the consulta leads to another ritual performance wherein the client propitiates a supernatural subject, asking for blessings and good fortune.

In the initiation of receiving the Warriors,[2] the neophyte learns a variety of new skills that will allow him to maintain the relationships he is forming with his godparents and the Warriors themselves. His elders wash his head and thus enact their authority over him and the religion's emphasis on the head as the bodily seat of individual spiritual power. Through participating in his first sacrifice, the neophyte "feeds" the orichas that protect him and learns basic skills about handling animals. He prostrates himself in moforibale, enacting his own subjugation to the authority of his elders and the orichas that empower their ritual acts. He leaves the ritual with the fundamentos of four orichas with whom he will likely interact weekly for the rest of his life, attending them with prayers, songs, and offerings of food. Depending on the ritual family to which he belongs, the neophyte may also be authorized to make blood sacrifice to his Warriors on his own behalf. Here the neophyte formalizes a relationship with authoritative human subjects and begins an intimate relationship with aggressive and protective oricha subjects, while learning key aspects of the religion through the body.

The asiento, the full initiation of a new priestess, permanently links the specific human subject to a particular supernatural one in uniquely complex yet patterned ways. Ritual elders repeatedly remove symbols and physical embodiments of the initiate's past identity and then reconstitute her in intimate and undeniable connection to her head-ruling oricha. Her oricha's advice provides her with previously unavailable guidance about the rest of her life, including personal taboos, areas of successful endeavor, and possible pitfalls in her character and relationships. Wise initiates refer to this new understanding again and again after their asientos, and all priestesses understand that they exist in a connective relationship with the orichas in which each party's actions deeply affect the other.

After a year as an initiate and the *ebó del año* (Lu., Sp. sacrifice of the year), the new priestess is authorized to lead many rituals on her own. She can participate in the initiation of other priests—singing songs for Osain, the oricha of herbs, and crowning them with the powerful herbal mixture that embodies the power of the gods. She can consult the orichas, divining their will for herself and others with either the coconut oracle or the cowrie shells that are the "mouths" of her orichas. She can sacrifice most animals to the gods to urge them to assist human beings. Although certain ritual performances are still out of her bounds,[3] the new priestess is so-cially authorized and at some basic level prepared to be a competent ritual performer who transforms the subjectivities of other humans.

When undergoing any initiation beyond the asiento, ritual perfor-mances authorize human subjects to perform certain roles in relation to other subjects, human and supernatural. Thus a priestess's subjectivity shifts in relation to various other subjects as she mediates between other humans and the gods, performs solely for the gods, and has other initiates perform rituals for her benefit. The subjective position of the priestess poses particularly interesting questions. How does she see her role? To what extent is that role a critical aspect of her sense of self, her personal identity? Which aspects of her subjectivity does she share with noninitiates? Which aspects does she share with fellow priests? Which genres does she deploy to communicate her subjectivity? And in which contexts? Answers to some of these questions emerge as priestesses and priests negotiate different commitments within a connective social system where no human subject is completely separate from its supernatural colleagues and individual independence is essentially impossible.

As priestesses and priests come to act as full members of the Santería community, they learn the principles of action that undergird the rituals that empowered them as ritual specialists and that structure their own performances. All practitioners gather what they learn from their elders and what they witness in rituals performed by others to forge their own particular vision of the religion; each practitioner stresses different aspects of the system, and each understands the generative power called aché in a slightly different way. Though priestesses and priests rarely articulate these principles or reflect upon them as theological and meta-physical tenets, they do invoke them at moments of social crisis to justify their actions in the face of criticism and gossip of their peers. As practitioners vie for social power, they argue for their perspective based on how they imagine the principles for action within the religion.

LIVED EXPERIENCE, PERFORMANCE, AND SUBJECTIVITY

The complexity of the lived experience of Santería practitioners can be effectively analyzed only in light of the performances of individuals who both inhabit social roles and experience those roles subjectively. To understand these people, this book has explored the diversity of ritual performances, bodily capacities, and competing social and ideological allegiances. In emphasizing issues of practice it has connected different ritual performances—divination, sacrifice, initiation, observing taboos, improvising rituals—by examining how more structural aspects of these ritual actions constitute and maintain the subjective presence of both humans and gods. It has also united two currents within anthropology—performance theory and the anthropology of experience—to apprehend and portray the social processes that create human agency and lived experience as well as the agency of the spirits in the religious field.

Beyond the performances and social processes that construct these subjectivities, it is possible to broaden the framework of understanding to include more differentiated notions of agency and subjectivity. The many related performances presented here provide only a limited glimpse into the lived experience of Santería practitioners because they focus on the classical dichotomy between the social given and individually experienced, what I have called the person and the self (Mauss's *moi*). Although this distinction has been fundamental to explorations of personhood for several generations of scholars, it is now possible further to differentiate aspects of agency and subjectivity.[4]

As adumbrated earlier, practitioners who have passed through higher levels of initiation possess a different sort of subjectivity from those who have not. This developmental aspect of subjectivity emerges frequently in the social world of the Santería religion when practitioners compare their "years in the religion" (Lu., Sp. *años en ocha*). Because of the hierarchical nature of the tradition, those practitioners with more years of initiation automatically have more autonomy and more authority than their younger counterparts. Their authority can be, and often is, undercut based on others' claims to ritual knowledge, but their position as elders remains secure, and they can demand service of various kinds from their juniors; the differing subjectivity of the elders can be seen as their juniors carry plates heaped with food and "throw" themselves before the elders.[5]

Just as levels of initiation distinguish one human subject from another, practitioners evaluate each other by applying the social norms of the religion to separate conforming and subversive agents. Integral to the discourse of the religion, gender and gendered positions play a central role in this process. Men and women have access to differing social positions and communicatively constituted and demonstrable social capacities; the most obvious example of this can be seen in Ifá practice, where women can enter and benefit from rituals but can never perform them. Outside of Ifá, however, practitioners extend traditional Cuban gender roles to the positions within the religion: elders encourage young men to pursue the position of oríaté; although this role is technically open to everyone, I have heard of only two women who have held it.[6] Most practitioners see these women as subversive or unusual at some level, despite their efficacy and knowledge as ritual specialists.

Similarly, homosexual men also occupy an important, if complicated, position within the religious system. Because the religion's initiations repeatedly deploy tropes of birthing, practitioners doubt the efficacy of any man not engaged in active procreation. However, because oricha priests are "taken" by the orichas in possession and because all initiates become the "younger wife" of the orichas, many Cubans and Cuban Americans assume that all oricha priests are gay—and, in reality, many are. This tension surfaces again and again in the discourse of the religion, and babalawos, members of the exclusively male and allegedly straight priesthood of the oricha Orula, often cite this tendency when criticizing oricha priests who threaten them in any way. Gay oricha priests subvert cultural norms about sexuality, but some compensate for their homosexuality's effects on their reputations by becoming severe and rigid about ritual matters.

Like gender and sexual preference, a practitioner's relationship with the spirits of the dead can also lead to subversive practices. The egun have diverse life histories, and they often ask their human charges to perform rituals based on those life stories—rituals outside of the norms of the tradition of the Regla de Ocha. The most provocative example of egun influence I have witnessed involved a Yemayá priest, whom I will call Rigoberto Sandoval, who was also a devotee of Hinduism. His Hindu tutelary spirit demanded that Sandoval routinely practice tantric meditation before an elaborate altar to the Hindu gods. After going broke and losing his home, Sandoval turned to Yemayá for assistance, and she responded that he needed to focus his attention on the orichas and on her if he was to succeed. A diviner who read the shells for Sandoval commented, "He's all over the place. He needs to decide if he wants to be Hindu or if he wants to be a santero. But now he knows what Yemayá wants." He continued saying that Sandoval needed to understand that the orichas have more authority than the spirits and that Sandoval needed to heed Yemayá's words. This brief account gives a sense of the effects—spiritual and social—that can arise when a spirit urges a priest to undertake unusual practices: the priest must choose between denying the spirit, subverting the social norms of agency, or finding some synthesis that balances these concerns.

Aside from developmental and subversive aspects of agency, the Santería religion offers rich resources to explore the internal and external influences that affect individual agents. In the life reading of the asiento, the orichas tell the initiate exactly what life circumstances will arise and what aspects of personal character will play an important role in the initiate's life. Some initiates understand all these characteristics as givens, as an inescapable destiny, and embrace the good and the bad as essential to their being. These practitioners later justify their socially destructive acts by referring back to the itá; it is common to hear phrases such as, "I am a child of Odí Meyi, so I am a womanizer by my sign."[7] Other initiates understand the itá as revealing character traits that will be present but do not have to be acted out. Miami oríaté Ernesto Pichardo has said that all traits of the odu from the head-ruling oricha become manifest at some point in a person's life; he thus combines the notion of development and the characteristics of the odu to make a profound assertion about the agency of initiated practitioners. For Pichardo, the characteristics of the odu form an inescapable destiny (Lu. *ipín,* Sp. *destino*), and the individual can choose how to deal with that destiny. Exploring agency in terms of internal and external influence leads directly to central ideas in the religion's psychological and theological systems.

Another key theological idea—secrecy—also reveals a great deal about different kinds of subjectivity in the religion. This text has already explored some of the contexts in which secrecy is invoked and some of its effects on social life, but in addition to heightened self- and social-awareness, secrecy results in practitioners internalizing discretion—a key cultural value. In fact, discretion has very real and powerful consequences for Santería practitioners. In a society where the pull of belonging to a family or religious community often overpowers any semblance of individuality, containing information about motives and goals effectively separates practitioners from those around them and provides them with the social space to act autonomously.

Secrecy has taken on a new dimension in recent years, as travel between Cuba and the United States has become more common. As practitioners with Cuban connections move between the United States and the island, they are often able to hide their activities on either side. This social secrecy allows them to access communities in Cuba of which their colleagues in the United States might not approve. Many of these practitioners have created parallel if unequal communities in both places, performing small ceremonies in the United States and larger, more extensive ones in Cuba, where the

costs are lower.[8] Similarly, practitioners have begun to create an almost un-
regulated religious domain on the World Wide Web. Several organizations
and individuals maintain an active Web presence. Though the Web has its
own dynamic, most practitioners use it as a way to reach more people and
thus extend their own charisma. Again the lack of social constraint has led
to misrepresentations about certain practitioners' knowledge, skill, religious authority, and social power. In every domain where secrecy manifests
itself, it affects people's subjectivity and their self-representation.

Certainly, then, Santería contains highly differentiated notions of the
human subject. Because the anthropological notion of agency involves in-
tentionality and action, autonomy and power, influence and interdependence, a full description of subjectivity in any culture would need to
explore how these issues play out. Is the possessed subject the same as the
everyday subject? How does the mediated agency of possession affect the
social world? What are the ideas that Santería practitioners have about
internal and external influences on themselves and others?[9]

Here cultural notions about fate and personality begin to color our explorations into agency and subjectivity, and "the *person* can now be
understood as a description of the cultural framework" of the subject (Pile
and Thrift 1995:9). Every person implies the simultaneously real, symbolic, and imaginary basis of his or her society and its cultures, and each
subject experiences different kinds of being. Despite the biological univer-
sals of human life, the communicatively constituted, cultured experience
of being human will always be different—both from culture to culture and
from person to person. An anthropology of agency and subjectivity docu-
ments and analyzes these differing constructs and the experience of subjectivity within them. In addition to exploring the lived experience of
particular subjects, it examines the local and historical construction of the
various tropes that structure subjectivity. To understand Santería practitioners as persons and to appreciate their experiences of living with the orichas, a cogent account of the social construction of subjectivity under
specific historical circumstances must describe how the religion instills its
particular moral imagination in its members and how those members negotiate their multiple motivations and interests. As Santería practitioners
make these choices, they reproduce certain inherent tensions between
classes of human subjects in the religion as well as transform the central
ritual practices that constitute and sustain the manifestations of the supernatural subjects.

One of these supernaturals, the oricha Ochún, recently visited me in a dream and explained. In the persons of Santería—their subjectivity, their ritual practices, and narratives about them, it is possible to sense the emergent qualities of being in the religion. Emergent human subjectivity highlights how people with complex commitments and real aspirations engage the world they have inherited from the elders. These subjects also have agency and often choose to act upon the world in unpredictable and impressive ways, transforming it and creating new possibilities for themselves and those who will follow them. "Dreams announce the possibility of another reality, and out of delirium emerges another kind of reason. What it all comes down to is that we are the sum of our efforts to change who we are" (Galeano 1991:125).

GLOSSARY

Abakuá An Afro-Cuban brotherhood originating among the Efik and Ejagham peoples of the Cross River delta of Nigeria.

abokú (Lu.) Lit. one who worships death; the name given to the neophyte during the early part of the initiation of an olocha.

aboricha (Lu.) Lit. one who worships the orichas; a name given to a person with a significant involvement in Santería but who has not been initiated as an olocha.

abuela de santo (Sp.) Lit. grandmother of the saint or holy grandmother; a woman who initiated a priestess or priest's godparent.

aché (Lu.) Generative power; performative skill; the power to accomplish; the inherent power that resides in all things.

aché de santo (Lu., Sp.) Generative power of the oricha, usually used to refer to the sacred herbs used in the initiation of an olocha.

acheces (Lu.) Essential parts of sacrificial animals that are cooked and offered to the orichas; always used in the plural.

acuaró (Lu.) Partridge.

adimú (Lu.) A small offering, usually comprising an oricha's favorite foods; also used in the expression *oricha de adimú* to refer to orichas whose sacred objects are received after an olocha's initiation.

adorar (Sp.) To worship or adore.

adurá (Lu.) Prayers.

ahijada (Sp.) Goddaughter; a girl or woman who has been initiated within an elder's ritual family.

ahijado (Sp.) Godson; a boy or man who has been initiated within an elder's ritual family.

ahijado de Guerreros   (Sp.) A godson who has received the Warriors within an elder's ritual family.

aleyo   (Lu.) Lit. stranger; a person just entering the religion; a person not affiliated with any ritual family.

años en ocha   (Lu., Sp.) Lit. years in oricha religion; an expression to identify the number of years since an olocha was initiated.

Arará   An Afro-Cuban ethnic identification for people and cultural elements tracing their roots to the region in Africa where Fon-speaking people live or the region formerly controlled by the Kingdom of Dahomey; also a rama or lineage of Santería with these same roots.

asiento   (Sp.) Lit. seating; name given to the initiation of a new priestess or priest.

ayé   (Lu.) World; the physical and visible world, usually contrasted with orun; also market.

babalawo   (Lu.) Lit. father of secrets; title of a priest of the oricha Orula.

babalocha   (Lu.) Lit. father of the oricha; a priest who has initiated another as an olocha; also called a santero.

Babalú-Ayé   Lucumí divinity of affliction, infectious diseases, and healing; usually imagined as an older man wondering about on crutches but sometimes as a king; often called *el viejo,* meaning "the old man" in Spanish.

batá   (Lu.) Sacred drums of the religion, animated by the oricha Añá.

batea   (Sp.) A wooden vessel housing the sacred objects of the oricha Changó.

bien hecha   (Sp.) Lit. well done; used to describe well-performed rituals.

bledo blanco   (Sp.) A sacred herb of great importance in the religion; called *lobé* in Lucumí and slender amaranth in English.

bo   (Lu.) To worship; root included in many Lucumí words, especially *ebó,* meaning a sacrificial offering.

borrar   (Sp.) To erase.

bóveda   (Sp.) Lit. a vault for the dead in a cemetery; name given to a domestic altar for ancestral spirits, usually influenced by European Spiritism.

buen corazón   (Sp.) Lit. good heart; used to describe those who express concern for others and do not allow their own interests to dominate social interactions.

cabeza   (Sp.) Lit. head; refers to the physical head, the individual person's spirit believed to reside there, and the principal deity.

cabildo   (Sp.) Mutual aid society, usually with an Afro-Cuban ethnic affiliation; widely considered to be the institution that forged the Santería religion as it exists today.

camino   (Sp.) Lit. road or journey; prospects or opportunities; implies course of life or destiny; appears in many proverbs, including *"cada cual vino al mundo con su propio camino"* (everyone came to the world with his own road), *"cuando se elige buen camino, se llega a la meta"* (when a good road is chosen, it ends at the goal), and *"cuando los caminos se cierran, sólo la* *inteligencia los abre"* (when the roads close, only intelligence will open them); also refers to different manifestations or avatars of the orichas.

Candomblé   Afro-Brazilian religion having similar origins to Santería and focused on the worship of many of the same deities; one of the source traditions for the Afro-Brazilian religion called Umbanda.

canto   (Sp.) Chant or sacred song that invokes, honors, and directs the orichas and the ancestral spirits; called *suyere* in Lucumí.

caracol   (Sp.) Lit. shell, often used in the plural *(caracoles)* to describe the cowrie shells that are the "mouths" of the deities.

casa   (Sp.) Lit. house; a religious community under the leadership of an elder or a group of elders.

cascarilla   (Sp.) Lit. little eggshell; a white chalk, often made from eggshell, used in many ceremonies as a purifying agent.

ceremonia   (Sp.) Ceremony.

ceremonia del río   (Sp.) Lit. ceremony of the river; the name of a key segment of the initiation of an olocha during which she visits the river to make sacrifice and be cleansed.

Changó   The powerful and regal oricha of thunder and justice; usually imagined as strong and virile; often called the king of the religion.

cliente   (Sp.) Client.

cocos   (Sp.) Lit. coconuts; a form of divination in which four pieces of coconut meat are cast and their pattern reveals that an oricha has accepted or rejected an offering; called *obí* in Lucumí.

coger   (Sp.) Lit. to take; used to describe how an oricha possesses a person and how a more active sexual partner engages a more passive one.

collar   (Sp.) Lit. necklace (plural *collares*); consecrated necklace in a specific pattern worn to connect a person to the oricha; describes a common and important ceremony—receiving the necklaces—in which new members of the religion receive the consecrated necklaces of key orichas; called *elekes* in Lucumí.

collar de mazo   (Sp.) Multistrand necklace used to adorn the sacred objects of the orichas, the bodies of those possessed by the orichas, and the bodies of new initiates.

congo   An Afro-Cuban ethnic identification for people and cultural elements tracing their roots to the Bantu-speaking areas in Africa; used to describe ancestral spirits with qualities associated with *congo* people, including physical strength, magical abilities, and rustic manners.

conocimiento   (Sp.) Understanding; used to describe a priest's or priestess's knowledge of the religion's history and ritual.

consulta   (Sp.) Consultation; used to describe a divination session.

cordobán   (Sp.) A sacred herb of great importance in the religion; called *peregún* in Lucumí and Moses-in-the-cradle in English.

coronación   (Sp.) Lit. coronation; the name of a key segment of the initiation of an olocha during which she is crowned with the orichas in various forms.

cuadro espiritual   (Sp.) Lit. spiritual portrait or spiritual symptoms; the group of ancestral spirits who accompany a person from birth to death.

cuchillo   (Sp.) Lit. knife; a ceremony that "confirms" the ritual authority given when a priest or priestess was originally consecrated, often interpreted as authorizing the use of a knife to sacrifice roosters and four-legged animals and enhancing the social independence of the priest or priestess.

culto   (Sp.) Lit. worship; the ceremonies performed in the worship of a particular oricha.

cumpleaños de santo   (Sp.) Lit. saint's birthday or holy birthday; an annual ceremony to commemorate the initiation of an olocha and to please the orichas.

de asiento   (Sp.) Of or related to the initiation of an olocha; usually describes a godparent, a ritual family, or ritual lineage.

de sangre   (Sp.) Of or related to blood family; often used to distinguish blood family from ritual family members.

de santo   (Sp.) Holy, sacred, blessed; of or related to the orichas themselves or the Santería religion as a whole; often describes substances and ritual family relationships.

derecho   (Sp.) Fee for ritual services; monetary offering included in a larger sacrifice; monetary offering made to the principal oricha of someone performing a ceremony.

despojo   (Sp.) Lit. stripping, shedding; a spiritual cleansing ritual to remove negative influences from a person's present and future life.

destino   (Sp.) Destiny, fate, destination, final outcome; appears in many proverbs, including *"cada persona tiene su propio destino"* (each person has his/her own destiny).

día del itá   (Lu., Sp.) Third day of the initiation ceremony for a new priestess or priest during which the orichas speak to the neophyte.

día del medio   (Sp.) Lit. the middle day; the second day of the initiation ceremony for a new priest or priestess during which the neophyte dresses as the principal oricha and greets visitors.

dilogún   (Lu.) Divination with sixteen cowrie shells; a shortened form of the Lucumí word for sixteen, *merindilogún;* called *caracol* or *caracoles* in Spanish.

ebó   (Lu.) An offering of any kind (plural *eboces*); an act of worship; a ceremony meant to praise the orichas, or ancestors, or urge them into action on behalf of their human followers.

ebó de entrada   (Lu., Sp.) Opening sacrifice in the process of initiating a new olocha.

ebó del año   (Lu., Sp.) Sacrifice made one year after the initiation of a new olocha.

ebó eyé   (Lu.) An animal sacrifice in which the life of the animal is given to the orichas or ancestors for human benefit; also called *ebó oto eye balé.*

ebó kere   (Lu.) An offering that is meant to spiritually cleanse a person; called a *despojo* in Spanish.

eborí eledá   (Lu.) A ritual including an offering to the spiritual head, usually meant to calm and balance a person's spirit; called *rogación de la cabeza* in Spanish.

egun   (Lu.) Ancestral spirit, from either ritual and blood families (plural *egunes*); spirit responsible for creating the religion as it exists today as evidenced by the proverb *"egun lobi ocha"* (the ancestors gave birth to oricha religion; called *espíritus* or *muertos* in Spanish.

eledá   (Lu.) The spirit of an individual that resides in the physical head.

Elegguá   The mischievous and irascible Lucumí divinity of destiny and communication; imagined as both a child and an old man; sometimes called *el vocero* (Sp. the spokesman) because he is the messenger for all the other spirits.

Elegguá Echú Oníkokó   A "road" of the messenger oricha Elegguá who assists olochas when they divine with cowrie shells.

eleke   (Lu.) Lit. necklace or necklaces; consecrated necklaces in specific patterns worn to connect a person to the orichas; describes a common and important ceremony—receiving the necklaces—in which new members of the religion receive the consecrated necklaces of key orichas; called *collar* in Spanish.

entendimiento   (Sp.) Understanding, judgment; describes a person's knowledge of the beliefs and practices of the religion; synonym of *conocimiento*.

eru   (Lu.) One of the four essential herbs in the sacred herbal mass called *aché de santo*, which is used to make a new olocha.

espíritu   (Sp.) Spirit; ancestral spirit of any kind.

ewe   (Lu.) Herb or herbs used for ritual purposes; called *hierba* or *yerba* in Spanish.

ewó   (Lu.) Taboos or ritual prohibitions given to a new olocha, usually governing behaviors, places, foods, and clothing to be avoided.

Eyeunle   A divination figure revealed in cowrie shell divination when eight cowries land with their serrated "mouths" up; usually speaks of an unstable and ill-at-ease situation, but is best defined within the context of an actual divination ceremony.

firma   (Sp.) Lit. signature; a pattern of colored circles used to invoke the orichas in very specific ceremonies; usually painted on the floor and head of a neophyte.

firmeza   (Sp.) Stability, steadiness, resolve; one of the fundamental forms of well-being requested from the spirits and orichas in most ceremonies.

fuerza   (Sp.) Physical strength; strength of character; one of the fundamental forms of well-being requested from the spirits and orichas in most ceremonies.

fundamento   (Sp.) Lit. foundation, basics, essentials; sacred objects for the orichas consecrated by elders and given to initiates in ceremonies; often used as an adjective in the phrase *de fundamento*, referring to something's origins within the tradition.

gitano   (Sp.) Lit. gypsy; a kind of ancestral spirit who usually sings and "reads cards" to divine.

gorrión   (Sp.) Lit. a kind of sparrow; Cuban slang for the blues.

gorro   (Sp.) A style of cap commonly worn by male olochas.

gringo   (Sp.) Outsider, foreigner.

Guerreros   (Sp.) Lit. warriors; the name given to the first group of orichas received by a person entering the religion; describes a common and important ceremony—receiving the Warriors—in which new members of the religion receive the sacred objects of the following orichas: Elegguá, Ogún, Ochosi, and Osun; called Oricha-Odé (orichas of the forest) in Lucumí.

güiro   (Sp.) A large gourd; the musical instrument made from this gourd and a net of beads; a ceremony when several of these instruments play to call the orichas, praise them, and urge them into action for human benefit.

hacer ebó   (Lu., Sp.) To make a sacrifice or an offering; to perform a ceremony.

hacer santo   (Sp.) Lit. to make saint or to make holy; to undergo or to perform the rituals that consecrate a new priest or priestess of the orichas; used in many variations, including *hizo santo* (she was initiated), *hice tu santo* (I made your oricha, I initiated you), and *tienes santo hecho* (you have oricha made, you are initiated).

hermano   (Sp.) Sibling.

hierba   (Sp.) Herb or herbs used for ritual purposes; called *ewe* in Lucumí.

hierro   (Sp.) Lit. iron; a hoe blade or other piece of metal struck with a stick as part of a güiro ceremony.

historia   (Sp.) Lit. story, history (plural *historias*); stories about the orichas and other sacred characters; sacred narratives; called *pataki* in Lucumí.

idé   (Lu.) A bracelet; either a simple metal bangle or a beaded bracelet; one of the attributes of the orichas that their followers wear.

Ifá   (Lu.) The divination system used by babalawos and employing either a divining chain or sixteen palm nuts; sometimes describes all knowledge of both the visible and invisible worlds.

igbodú   (Lu.) Sacred room or space where a ceremony is performed and into which only those who have undergone that same ceremony can enter.

igüoro   (Lu.) An initiate; a priestess or priest; an olocha.

ilé   (Lu.) Lit. house; a religious community under the leadership of an elder or a group of elders; also lit. the earth.

ipín   (Lu.) Destiny, fate; called *camino* or *destino* in Spanish.

iré   (Lu.) Blessings or good luck.

Iroso Meyi   A divination figure revealed in cowrie shell divination when four cowries land with their serrated "mouths" up two times in a row; usually refers to a situation with many obstacles, but is best defined within the context of an actual divination ceremony.

itá   (Lu.) The ceremony when the orichas speak to their newly initiated follower;

a divination ceremony whose results are considered to reveal the destiny of the individual; usually involving more than one oricha and in the context of consecrating a new olocha.

italero (Lu., Sp.) The diviner who performs the itá; also called *oríaté*.

iyalocha (Lu.) Lit. mother of the oricha; a priestess who has initiated another as an olocha; also called *santera*.

iyawó (Lu.) Lit. younger wife; term used to designate a newly consecrated priest or priestess for the first year after initiation.

jutía (Sp.) A large rodent native to the Caribbean, called nutria in English; frequently used in sacrifices; offered live and in a powdered form after being smoked.

kariocha (Lu.) Name given to the initiation of a new priestess or priest; called *asiento* or *hacer santo* in Spanish.

kola (Lu.) Kola nut; one of the four essential herbs in the sacred herbal mass called *aché de santo* used to make a new olocha.

kuanaldo (Lu.) A ceremony that "confirms" the ritual authority given when a babalawo, or priest of Orula, was originally consecrated, often interpreted as authorizing the use of a knife to sacrifice roosters and four-legged animals and enhancing the social independence of the priest.

lavatorio (Sp.) Lit. washing; the name of a key segment of the initiation of an olocha during which the sacred objects of the orichas are washed in osain as part of their consecration.

limpio (Sp.) Clean, pure, without ulterior motives.

linda (Sp.) Beautiful, harmonious, producing a sense of well-being; used to describe ceremonies.

lo interior (Sp.) Physical insides, inner organs; inner life.

lobé (Lu.) A sacred herb of great importance in the religion; called *bledo blanco* in Spanish and slender amaranth in English.

Lucumí The liturgical language used in Santería with origins in the West African language Yoruba; comes from the Afro-Cuban ethnic identification for people and cultural elements tracing their roots to the region in Africa where Yoruba-speaking people live or lived.

macho (Sp.) Male, masculine; a man who is very assertive and strong.

maferefún oricha (Lu.) A common phrase used to praise or thank the orichas.

malanga (Sp.) A plant whose leaves are used in the ceremony to consecrate a new olocha.

matanza (Sp.) Slaughter; blood sacrifice; a key segment of the initiation rites for a new priestess or priest.

mayor (Sp.) Elder (plural *mayores*).

mi gente (Sp.) Lit. my people; people close or loyal to the speaker; an expression of solidarity.

misa espiritual   (Sp.) Lit. spiritual mass; a common ceremony from Spiritism that invokes and works with ancestral spirits.

mo dupe o   (Lu.) Lit. I give thanks; an exclamation of thanksgiving.

moforibale   (Lu.) A prostration performed to honor ritual elders and the oricha.

montaje del santo   (Sp.) Lit. mounting of oricha; a key segment in the initiation ritual of a new olocha.

montar   (Sp.) To mount; used to describe how an oricha possesses a practitioner.

mortal   (Sp.) Lit. mortal; in contemporary Cuban youth culture, describes an amazing or outstanding person.

moyuba   (Lu.) A prayer of invocation named for the repeated phrase *mo yuba,* meaning "I pay homage to" or "I show reverence for."

muerto   (Sp.) Lit. dead (plural *muertos*); the spirit of a dead person, an ancestral spirit; often juxtaposed with the orichas; called *egun* in Lucumí.

nangareo   (Lu.) A food made of cornmeal and water, sometimes from a corn tamale that is then mixed into water; a ceremony to prepare for itá, in which this food is offered.

obá   (Lu.) King; a common part of names for children of the oricha Changó.

Obara-Eyeunle   A divination figure revealed in cowrie shell divination when six cowries land with their serrated "mouths" up and then eight land in the same position in the following cast; frequently refers to a person surrounded by difficulties and unable to act, but best defined within the context of an actual divination ceremony.

Obara-Odí   A divination figure revealed in cowrie shell divination when six cowries land with their serrated "mouths" up and then seven land in the same position in the following cast; frequently refers to a person having difficulties making important decisions but best defined within the context of an actual divination ceremony.

Obara-Ogbe   Another name for the divination figure Obara-Eyeunle.

Obatalá   The merciful, wise, and calm Lucumí divinity responsible for creating the human body before birth and charged with overseeing all the other divinities' activities; usually imagined as an old man dressed in immaculate white cloth; often called *Babá* (father).

obí   (Lu.) Lit. coconut; a form of divination in which four pieces of coconut meat are cast on the floor and their pattern reveals that an oricha has accepted or rejected an offering; called *cocos* in Spanish.

Ocán Oñí   Lit. heart of honey; the author's name within the Santería religion.

Ocana-Odí   A divination figure revealed in cowrie shell divination when one cowrie lands with its serrated "mouth" up and then seven land in the same position in the following cast; frequently refers to a hard-headed and disoriented person, but best defined within the context of an actual divination ceremony.

Oché-Iroso   A divination figure revealed in cowrie shell divination when five cowries land with their serrated "mouths" up and then four land in the same position in the following cast; frequently refers to a person who must work hard to find success, but best defined within the context of an actual divination ceremony.

Oché-Metanlá   A divination figure revealed in cowrie shell divination when five cowries land with their serrated "mouths" up and then thirteen land in the same position in the following cast; frequently refers to a person who faces grave danger from infectious disease, but best defined within the context of an actual divination ceremony.

Oché-Meyi   A divination figure revealed in cowrie shell divination when five cowries land with their serrated "mouths" up two times in a row; usually refers to a situation with many ups and downs, but is best defined within the context of an actual divination ceremony.

Oché-Odí   A divination figure revealed in cowrie shell divination when five cowries land with their serrated "mouths" up and then seven land in the same position in the following cast; frequently refers to a person who faces danger from envy and witchcraft but best defined within the context of an actual divination ceremony.

Oché-Ojuani   A divination figure revealed in cowrie shell divination when five cowries land with their serrated "mouths" up and then eleven land in the same position in the following cast; frequently refers to a person who does not respect social norms and becomes ill, but best defined within the context of an actual divination ceremony.

ochinchín   (Lu.) An omelet offered to the oricha Ochún.

Ochosi   The solitary and reflective Lucumí divinity of the woods and hunting; usually imagined moving silently through the woods with a bow and arrow; often called *el cazador* (Sp. the hunter).

Ochún   The sensual and joyous Lucumí divinity of the river, love, and fortune; usually imagined as a beautiful young woman with honey-colored skin; often called *Yalorde*, a title for a powerful woman.

Odí Meyi   A divination figure revealed in cowrie shell divination when seven cowries land with their serrated "mouths" up two times in a row; usually refers to a situation of great extremes and passions but best defined within the context of an actual divination ceremony.

odu   (Lu.) Any divination figure generated through the coconuts, the cowries, the divining chain, or the palm nuts.

Ogún   The intense and often violent Lucumí divinity of iron and war; usually imagined as a physically powerful and bulky man with dark skin; often called *el herrero* (Sp. the blacksmith).

ogún   (Lu.) Medicine, usually in the form of powdered herbs.

Ogunda-Odí   A divination figure revealed in cowrie shell divination when three cowries land with their serrated "mouths" up and then seven land in the same position in the following cast; frequently refers to a person at war with others, but best defined within the context of an actual divination ceremony.

Ojuani   A divination figure revealed in cowrie shell divination when eleven cowries land with their serrated "mouths" up; frequently refers to a person operating without the necessary psychological, practical, or spiritual resources, but best defined within the context of an actual divination ceremony.

Oké   The solid and steady oricha of hills and mountains who works closely with Obatalá.

olocha   (Lu.) One belonging to or having the oricha; the title of anyone who has undergone the initiation ceremony called *asiento* or *kariocha*.

oloricha   (Lu.) A longer version of the term *olocha*.

Olorun   (Lu.) Lit. owner of heaven; one of the names of the High God who created the earth.

oluo   (Lu.) Lit. lord; a babalawo who was an olocha before being initiated into the priesthood of Orula.

omí   (Lu.) Water, a common ingredient in sacrifices and herbal preparations in the religion.

omiero   (Lu.) Lit. water of remedy; a mixture of herbal preparations or osaines made for different orichas.

omoricha   (Lu.) Lit. child of the oricha; a person with some commitment to the orichas; usually a person who has received the necklaces or the Warriors.

ópele   (Lu.) A chain with eight concave disks used by babalawos for divining.

orí   (Lu.) Lit. head; refers to the physical head, the individual person's spirit believed to reside there, and sometimes the principal deity.

orí inú   (Lu.) Lit. inner head; the individual's spirit believed to reside inside the physical head.

oríaté   (Lu.) A knowledgeable and senior priest or priestess who acts as a master of ceremonies, leading other olochas in performing initiations and other complicated eboces; sometimes called *italero*.

oricha   (Lu.) Divinity or deity belonging to the Afro-Cuban pantheon with origins in West African, Yoruba-speaking cultures; one of the many faces of the creator god Olodumare.

oriki   (Lu. and Yoruba) Salutations, praise poems or panegyrics; songs to call the orichas.

oro egun   (Lu.) A ceremony, including a cycle of chants, to honor the ancestral spirits.

Orula   The wise and measured Lucumí divinity of order and the Ifá divination system; often referred to as the judge of the orichas because he can be called on to resolve disputes.

orun   (Lu.) Heaven; the spiritual and invisible world, usually contrasted with ayé; also sky and sun.

osain (Lu.) Herbal preparation used to consecrate objects and people (plural *osaines*); medicine; linked to Osain, the divinity of herbs.

Osain The Lucumí deity of herbs and medicine.

osun (Lu.) Camwood; one of the four essential herbs in the sacred herbal mass called *aché de santo*, which is used to make a new olocha; also the Lucumí word for *firma*.

Osun A protective Lucumí deity who warns practitioners when they are in danger, associated with Osain, the deity of herbs and medicine; one of the Warriors.

otá (Lu.) Stone or rock consecrated to become the sacred objects of the orichas (plural *otanes* or *otaces*).

Oyá The turbulent and forceful warrior Lucumí deity of wind and storms; usually imagined as a strong-willed woman with a lot of attitude; sometimes called *Yansan*, a title linking her to the ancestral spirits.

oyubona (Lu.) The second godparent at a major initiation such as the asiento.

padrino (Sp.) Godparent; elder who has initiated others in the religion.

Palo Mayombe An Afro-Cuban religion with its primary origins in Bantu-speaking cultures in Central Africa; sometimes called Regla de Congo or Palo Monte.

Palo Monte See Palo Mayombe.

pañuelo (Sp.) Decorative cloth in the colors of a specific oricha, used on altars.

pasar (Sp.) To pass; describes human action when ancestral spirits manifest in possession.

patakí (Lu.) Lit. important story; stories about the orichas and other sacred characters; sacred narratives; called *historia* in Spanish.

peonía (Sp.) A sacred herb of great importance in the religion; called *wereyeye* in Lucumí and peony in English.

peregún (Lu.) A sacred herb of great importance; called *cordobán* in Spanish and Moses-in-the-cradle in English.

pinaldo (Lu.) A ceremony that "confirms" the ritual authority given when a priest or priestess was originally consecrated, often interpreted as authorizing the use of a knife to sacrifice roosters and four-legged animals and enhancing the social independence of the priest or priestess.

protector (Sp.) Protective ancestral spirit (plural *protectores*).

rama (Sp.) Lit. branch; a group of related religious houses tracing their relationships and usually their ritual practices back in time to the same ancestor or group of ancestors; a spiritual lineage with ritual norms.

recopilación (Sp.) Compilation; gathering information on religious history and ritual practices as a road to greater knowledge and usually greater authority.

refrán (Sp.) Proverb; conventional wisdom related to different divination figures.

registrado (Sp.) Lit. searched; the person for whom a divination ceremony is performed; the object of the revelations.

Regla de Ocha   An Afro-Cuban religion with its primary origins in Yoruba-speaking cultures in West Africa; also called Santería.

Regla Kimbisa   A revitalization movement attempting to merge the three most prominent Afro-Cuban religions (Santería, Palo Monte, and Abakuá) with astrology and numerology; claims few practitioners today.

rogación de la cabeza   (Sp.) Lit. prayer for the head; a ritual including an offering to the spiritual head, usually meant to calm and balance a person's spirit; called *eborí eledá* in Lucumí.

rompimiento   (Sp.) Lit. breaking; a spiritual cleansing ritual to remove negative influences from a person's present and future life and generally including the ritual destruction of the clothes the person is wearing.

rubó   (Lu.) To make a sacrifice or an offering; see *ebó*.

salud   (Sp.) Physical health, well-being; one of the fundamental forms of blessing requested from the spirits and orichas in most ceremonies.

San Lázaro   Saint Lazarus, whom Jesus raised from the dead in the Bible; closely associated with the Lucumí divinity Babalú-Ayé; a name used to avoid invoking Babalú-Ayé by accident.

santera   (Sp.) A priestess of the orichas; the title of a woman who has undergone the initiation ceremony called *asiento* or *kariocha*; a generic name for a woman who is either an olocha or an iyalocha.

Santería   An Afro-Cuban religion with its primary origins in Yoruba-speaking cultures in West Africa; also called Regla de Ocha or simply Ocha; sometimes referred to in English as the Oricha religion.

santero   (Sp.) A priest of the orichas; the title of a man who has undergone the initiation ceremony called *asiento* or *kariocha*; a generic name for man who is either an olocha or a babalocha.

santo   (Sp.) Lit. holy or saint; used to describe consecrated objects and sacred spaces; used by some as a synonym for *oricha*.

señora   (Sp.) Lady; ma'am.

sentimiento   (Sp.) Feeling or sentiment; often contrasted with *conocimiento* or *entendimiento* (Sp. understanding or knowledge).

serio   (Sp.) Serious; a serious student of the religion; one dedicated to gathering and using knowledge about religious history and ritual practices.

sin interés   (Sp.) Without interest or ulterior motives; selfless.

suerte   (Sp.) Luck, opportunity, fortune; one of the fundamental forms of blessing requested from the spirits and orichas in most ceremonies.

suyere   (Lu.) Chant or sacred song that invokes, honors, and directs the orichas and the ancestral spirits; called *canto* in Spanish.

tambor   (Sp.) Lit. a drum; a ceremony in which drums play to call the orichas, praise them, and urge them into action for human benefit; often called a drumming in English.

toque (Sp.) Lit. beat, playing of an instrument; another name for a ceremony when musical instruments are played to call the orichas.

trabajo (Sp.) Lit. work; an offering or sacrifice usually requesting a specific outcome in the physical world.

traje del almuerzo (Sp.) Lit. Lunch costume or dress; clothes worn by a neophyte on the morning of the middle day of the initiation of priestess or priest.

trono (Sp.) Lit. throne; a large, three-dimensional cloth altar in which the sacred objects of the orichas rest for important ceremonies.

tú (Sp.) You, in the familiar form.

Umbanda An Afro-Brazilian religion sharing some of the origins of Santería and focused on the worship of ancestral spirits linked to many of the same deities; a religion related to Candomblé.

usted (Sp.) You, in the formal form.

vencimiento de todas las dificultades (Sp.) Overcoming of all difficulties; one of the fundamental forms of blessing requested from the spirits and orichas in most ceremonies.

wereyeye (Lu.) A sacred herb of great importance in the religion; called *peonía* in Spanish and peony in English.

Yalorde (Lu.) A title given to a powerful woman, usually reserved to honor the divinity of the river, Ochún.

Yemayá The majestic and maternal Lucumí divinity of the sea and motherhood; usually imagined as a dark-skinned woman with children and a strong temper; sometimes called "the first oricha to come to the defense of humanity."

yerba (Sp.) Herb or herbs used for ritual purposes; called *ewe* in Lucumí.

yo (Sp.) I.

NOTES

INTRODUCTION: *Living Santería*

1. The term *Afro-Cuban* is a simple handle that recalls the origins and history of these practices and the people who created them. By its use I do not mean to suggest that the culture is limited to people of African descent or to Cuba, although it does seem to have the deepest roots there.

2. In recent years, several influential ritual leaders in Santería have sought to take titles in the academy. Miguel "Willie" Ramos and Ysamur Flores have both written for academic honors after long careers as powerful practitioners.

3. J. Fabian (1983) has argued that using the present tense to describe living people deprives them of history and suggests that they are unchanging. I am aware of this danger, but I use the present tense in narrative precisely to draw readers into the action, just as novelists sometimes do.

4. This short discussion cannot resolve the tensions that exist in anthropology between scientific and humanistic approaches to the study of human life. Instead, it attempts to locate this ethnography for the reader.

5. *Aboricha* seems to be relatively new in Cuban circles and may have been introduced by African-American omoricha as they sought to expand the African sources of the religion.

6. For an excellent, short description of Afro-Cuban oricha religion, see Ramos 1996.

7. Omoricha believe this is true of all people, regardless of their involvement in the culture. This systematic inclusiveness is one factor that has helped accelerate the religion's spread.

8. See González-Wippler 1989:229 for an insider's exploration of these psycho-divine correspondences. These correspondences are problematic inasmuch as the ruling deity can compensate for the person's character (see Gleason 1987:259–272).

9. For an extended discussion of the sexual implications of mounting in Brazil, see Wafer 1991.

10. See Murphy 1981 for an exposition of this schematic notion of the workings of the religion. Omoricha of the religion turn to divination to reveal the desires of the spirits and their individual destinies. Four pieces of coconut (Lu. *obí,* Sp. *cocos),* cowrie shells

(Lu. *dilogún,* Sp. *caracoles*), and palm nuts (Lu. *Ifá*) are all used in different but related systems.

11. *Santería* is a Spanish word meaning "the process of making saints," whereas *Regla de Ocha* is a mixture of Spanish and Lucumí and means "the rule of the divinities." Santería is the name more commonly used by outsiders, but followers of the religion usually call it by its African name, Ocha or Oricha. The name used for the religion has become an issue of hot debate in recent years as Cubans, Cuban Americans, Africans, African Americans, and some leading Euro-American practitioners have all articulated different names, each implying and stressing certain histories, loyalties, and ideologies.

12. See Mbiti 1975 on the general structure of African religions.

13. At this moment, many voices claim authority to narrate the complex historical process that created this nexus of beliefs and practices. For one schematic overview of the historical process that created the religion as it exists today, see Murphy 1988 and 1994: 81–113. For a detailed account of the history of aesthetic practices within the religion, see D. Brown 1989. Brandon's 1993 account of the history is by far the most comprehensive, and although the historical material is problematic because it remains too general and schematic, he provides some valuable information about the religion as it is practiced by African Americans.

14. In this text, I have written about many aspects of the religion that are not usually detailed so clearly to outsiders, although other books provide more specific ritual information. See, for example, Angarica 1955, Brandon 1983, D. Brown 1989, Cabrera 1980, Mason 1985, and Ramos 1982.

15. These blessings are routinely requested at every ceremony and represent a set of core values to which individuals aspire within the religion. It should be noted that these core values unite a tremendous diversity of practices by practitioners who model their actions on traditional lineages called *ramas* (Sp. lit. branches).

16. In fact, the self in some form has preoccupied much of Western intellectual history and philosophy. The Greeks' concern with self-knowledge reflects a similar concern (Mamigliano 1985), even if the Greek self was not closely related to our definitions (Smith 1985:67–69). To jump forward in time, Kant's dualistic self emphasized the fact that persons are both subjects *and* objects in social life—an idea that greatly influenced Mauss (1938), the symbolic interactionists, and therefore our current understandings of the self (see Goffman 1959, 1974). The Romantics elaborated the mysterious and independent self as the center of their philosophy and literature, and they concluded that only through separation from the harmful effects of society could the true self emerge (Whittaker 1992). This Romantic, hidden self attracted Freud and his successors as they tried to plumb the "depths" of the personal unconscious. It survives in the discourse of psychoanalysis and psychology today.

17. See Drewal 1992 on the trope of journeys in Yoruba culture in West Africa. Footnotes throughout this text make reference to parallel material in West African and African Diaspora ethnography.

18. The term *subject* comes from the structuralist and poststructuralist schools of thought that have greatly influenced linguistics, psychoanalysis, feminism, philosophy, and social theory, especially in the last two decades. For a good summary of its history, see Pile and Thrift 1995.

19. Although an external authority demarcates the individual from others, this conception

has a long and distinguished history in Western philosophical thought (Lukes 1980). Although frequently linked to the person, the individual often merits consideration simply because he or she is an individual and therefore separate from other individuals (Whittaker 1992:198). Other discourses on the individual have used the term *man* to explore the nature and dynamics of the person. I am not interested in pursuing the questions of this particular discourse on the individual, though I am fully aware that it has greatly influenced my own discourse of subjectivity. *Character, personality,* and *mind* have also played important roles in the psychological discourses that address subjectivity; see Whittaker 1992.

20. Though not integral to this discussion, the subject also implicates the unconscious as an aspect of all individuals' lives at both the structural and subjective levels.

1. "THE BLOOD THAT RUNS THROUGH THE VEINS": *Defining Identity and Experience in Dilogún Divination*

1. A transcription and translation of this divination session can be found in Mason 1992.

2. Although some diviners disagree about the proverbs that accompany specific figures, Oché seems to be associated universally with this proverb. For examples where the same figure carries different proverbs, see Ecún 1988:131 versus González-Wippler 1989:130.

3. Many references evidence this fact. David Brown (1989:369) discusses sacrifices to free people from jail and others that must be performed at a police station or a courthouse, and Obá Ecún (1988:37, 89) gives several small sacrifices (Lu. *adimú*) for freeing prisoners. The causes of this phenomenon deserve future research.

4. It is interesting to note here that divination can be seen as a quintessential negotiation between structure and agency. The shells speak through the diviner; the figure that appears refers to traditional materials and interpretations, and the client either accepts or rejects this understanding of the situation. This reading of the ritual, of course, examines only the structural interaction of the diviner and the client while ignoring the larger traditional frame of the ritual itself.

5. Jackson's work on radical empiricism suggests using the ethnographer's experience as primary data (1989:4). I have offered this information as an addition to the other data presented here.

6. That I feel as if I have been seen by another person after retelling the stories of my life is in no way surprising. Sandra Dolby-Stahl has argued forcefully that the personal experience narrative functions frequently to create intimacy (see Dolby-Stahl 1977, 1989:37–43).

7. See Munn 1973 on the ritual structuring of personal experience.

8. See Leder 1990, which argues that the dichotomy is in fact based on an empirical experience of self. This argument's refreshing and clear position emerges from its empirical approach.

9. I have used the occasion of this chapter on the experience of the client of dilogún divination to express the possibility of reflective flow. The idea emerged over a long period of time as I reflected on my own experiences of important rituals in my own life. The issue as it appears here and applies to an anthropology of experience was greatly clarified through repeated conversations with Rory P. B. Turner, whose help and friendship I gratefully acknowledge.

10. See Bascom 1980:35 for the Yoruba view of destiny and its relationship to divination. See also Murphy 1981, which posits this relationship as fundamental to the ritual system of Santería.

11. This interpretation of sacrifice only works for the consulta; other sacrifices are made in the Regla de Ocha that are not structurally related to catharsis. The best example is the large annual sacrifices on the anniversary of initiation; see D. Brown 1989:419–432.

12. It is important to notice that María follows the general intent of the diviner's instructions but alters the form of the sacrifice to the goddess. Instead of returning to him, she alters the sacrifice and offers Ochún other foods that she likes. This alteration of tradition can be seen as a resistance to the oríaté's position of power: Although María accepts the information that she receives from him, she chooses to perform a private sacrifice that does not include him. María explains, "I did offer Ochún some oranges and some chocolate chip cookies and some candles. . . . I just told her [Ochún] that I had somehow made a promise to her that I hadn't kept and that I was trying to keep my promise, which is what he [José] said. . . . I did it to show my respect. I took it to be a serious moment" (Hernández 1991).

2. "I BOW MY HEAD TO THE GROUND": *Creating Bodily Experience through Initiation*

1. I witnessed the ritual described here in December 1990. Since 1988 I have worked extensively with the community that performed the ceremony. This group of practitioners is led by Cuban priests and priestesses but includes people of various social, economic, and cultural backgrounds. Because of this diversity I have limited my analysis to the religious system. I have also limited the detailed personal information about the participants. Santería is still not widely accepted, and so these people have asked that I not make their identities public or recognizable. I created a pseudonym for each person and used it consistently throughout the book.

2. "The road in the saint" is a common expression in Santería that refers to a person's destiny in the religion. This initiation is referred to as "receiving the Warriors."

3. Certainly ritual does not simply "reflect" the entire culture (cf. Benedict 1935), but it does provide a useful and edifying entry point for cultural analysis.

4. I plan to explore these valuative, aesthetic categories in future work.

5. For an extended discussion of the sexual implications of mounting in Brazil, see Wafer 1991.

6. Carter has been involved in this ritual house since before I started studying it. He, like most new American practitioners, has a mixture of book learning and practical experience within the religion. I am not certain where he learned the prayer to which he refers here.

7. I have not described the Osun ritual because in the house that I am studying I was asked not to divulge it; for a similar ritual, see Murphy 1988. There are interesting correlations between Ocha's emphasis on the head and Vodou ritual practice; see K. Brown 1991:67, 350–351.

8. "The head carries the body" is an often quoted proverb (Sp. *refrán*) that is associated with the divination figure called Eyeunle, which is ruled by the white deity Obatalá, the owner of all heads.

9. It is worth noting that a priestess present at the ritual also squeezed the air from the rooster when it squealed. Thus, this particular instance does not represent the acquisi-

tion of gendered behavior. It seems probable that an investigation of Santería and gender would be helped by this rich ethnographic example where a man gives *"macho"* (Sp. masculine, male) divinities to another man. It should be noted that women also receive the Guerreros, and always from a man.

10. The word *moforibale* is Lucumí, and its translation is revealing: It is an elision of the phrase *mo fi orí ba ilé. Mo* is the first person pronoun "I"; *fi* is an operative marking indicating the use of something, in this case *orí,* "the head." *Ba* is the verb "to touch," and *ilé* is "the ground" or "the earth." Thus, a more literal translation would be "I use my head to touch the ground."

11. Ritual kin, relatives *de santo,* are usually contrasted by practitioners with blood kin, relatives *de sangre* (Sp. of blood).

12. In fact, the moforibale is performed in many other contexts as a form of respect. Most important, it is done in front of elaborate altars called *tronos* (Sp. thrones) that are offered to the orichas. See Friedman 1982:198–214 for a lengthy discussion of mutual respect in Santería. See D. Brown 1989, especially chapters 5 and 7, for excellent and extended discussions of tronos and the attendant rituals of respect. See also D. Brown 2003.

13. It is important to note that George is not thoroughly separating the orichas and his ritual elders. When he does moforibale, he is technically honoring the physical orichas as well as the orichas that are crowned in the heads of the elders. David Brown (1989: 170–171) quotes Melba Carrillo, an oloricha in New Jersey, as reiterating that the moforibale salutes the *"oricha* crowned on the head of the person, not the person." George's experience of the ritual does not include this highly differentiated semantic meaning for the moforibale.

3. "MY PANTS ARE BLOODY": *Negotiating Identity in American Santería*

1. Two chickens were sacrificed to the dead in fulfillment of cowrie shell divination that had revealed that the dead were helping the initiate. A rooster, three pigeons, and a Guinea hen were shared by the Warriors. See chapter 2 for a detailed discussion of the ritual initiation of receiving the Warriors.

2. Most Cuban Americans, though still closely connected to life in Cuba, do not expect to return to their homeland. Yet most of them are not interested in assimilating into American culture. More than most ethnic groups of the past, Cubans in the United States appear to remain in ethnic enclaves longer and learn English more slowly than other groups (Pedraza-Bailey 1985:4). Despite widespread integration into the political and economic spheres of life in the United States, Cuban Americans seem unwilling to submit to cultural assimilation. This trend seems to be tapering off with those born in the United States after the late 1960s.

3. This derecho greatly exceeds those charged by most priests. At the time, the average derecho for receiving the Warriors in Washington, D.C., was $275, and it was similar in major areas like Miami and New York City. The current rate in Washington, D.C., is between $300 and $450, although some charge as much as $1,200. These higher prices reflect personal economies dependent entirely on income from the religion.

4. It is imperative to stress that the ontological reality of these selves is debatable. There does exist a more "singular" José that is bounded and contained by skin. This physical self, for our purposes, represents another distinct self whose role in this individual's life remains

somewhat unclear. For an interesting exposition of some of the possible selves that exist in a life, see John Elster's excellent introduction to *The Multiple Self* (1986:1–34).

5. I have intentionally reused this section of the first chapter, with very minor changes, to emphasize that the oríaté, an important and respected ritual specialist, and the client of a divination session have many of the same selves and many capacities in common.

6. See D. Brown 1989:377–478 for an excellent discussion of the aesthetics of thrones in the religion.

7. The idea of an individual with multiple persons seems to imply an infinite regress of persons—what are more conventionally called selves. That is, if every self is multiple, then selves have selves that in turn have selves (see Ogilvy 1977, chapter 3). If considered as different aspects of agency relevant to a single human subject, then that subject can still be unified, an idea very dear to humanist philosophers.

8. I collected this narrative from the famous oríaté Santiago Pedroso in Philadelphia in late December 1987; he quoted it in reference to the divination figure called Ojuani-Odí, although I have never found it in written sources on divination.

9. José no longer works or lives in the Washington, D.C., area.

4. LIVING WITH THE ORICHAS: *Ritual and the Social Construction of the Deities*

1. This spelling of *oricha* represents the standard in Yoruba. Because the information in this section integrates religious practices from around the Atlantic world to elucidate the Afro-Cuban species, I have chosen to maintain the Cuban spelling in my analysis of these materials.

2. This insightful analysis overlooks the *orí inú*, the inner head, which one receives before birth and usually contains ancestral being (Bascom 1991:116; Morakinyo and Akiwowo 1981). Thus, for many people this ancestral self receives the oricha presence as a supplement or as a "crown."

3. This translation is mine.

4. Throughout this section I refer to the neophyte as a woman, because the majority of initiates are women. Women enter the religion in greater numbers than men for a great number of different reasons, including historical precedent and gender roles. This issue requires additional research. For ease of contrast I have made the godparents men, although this is by no means always the case.

5. In 1995, the asiento briefly described at the beginning of this section cost upward of ten thousand Cuban pesos. An established medical doctor in Cuba earns approximately four thousand pesos per year. In Cuba the price varies with the cost of animals and other ingredients; these are affected by the hard currency exchange rate.

6. *Babalocha,* Lucumí for father of the oricha, is the term for men.

7. Although I have explained the reasons behind using certain ingredients in some cases, I have to a large degree avoided the question because it is not relevant to my argument.

8. In some houses this task belongs to the *babalawos* (Lu.), priests of Orula. In these houses the babalawos also perform the major sacrifice.

9. Coconut divination, called *obí* in Lucumí and *cocos* in Spanish, is quite common in the religion to determine the outcome of sacrifices. There are five basic variations that can come out, and each one leads to a particular course of action in the ceremony. Many practitioners have written manuals to explain how to do this kind of divination; for an excellent example see Ramos 1982.

10. The idea of doing penance appears in a number of Santería ceremonies. Although the term clearly comes from Roman Catholicism, these ritual interludes do not reflect a need to pay for sins. Rather, they are quiet and introverted moments in a gregarious culture.

11. Throughout the initiation of a new priestess, the assembled community of oricha worshipers intones songs whose performances are essential to the ceremony. This more structurally oriented chapter does not include transcriptions or analyses of these songs, which I hope to address in future work.

12. This ceremony also stresses the subjectivity of the orichas. Oríatés Ernesto Pichardo in Miami and Saúl Fernández in Havana both agree that this casting of the cowries is the newborn orichas prostrating themselves to the earth (Lu. *ilé*) on which they will live. In the funerary rites of the religion, the orichas again prostrate themselves in a single casting before leaving the earth.

13. *Santo* can be translated as *saint,* but it can also mean *holy* or *sacred.* In normal Cuban usage, to ask for the saint one would say *el santo.*

14. Certain orichas do not go to the head for various reasons, and the oríaté places these on the shoulders or nape of the neck.

15. See chapter 2.

16. See Brandon 1990 for a presentation of the songs as examples of Africanisms in the United States. His transcriptions are identical to the song lyrics presented in John Mason's 1985 well-explained ritual manual.

17. This word is the plural of aché, meaning the power to accomplish. This fact suggests that these body parts somehow contain the most critical power of the animal, although most practitioners do not explain this fascinating coincidence.

18. For more detailed information about the different garments used in the asiento, see D. Brown 1989 and 1993; Flores 1990; Flores and Evanchuk 1994.

19. With the exception of following issues through several readings with different orichas, these consultations with the orichas resemble others (see M. Mason 1993).

20. This part of the ritual is done less as practitioners become more conscious of the African origin of the religion and less tolerant of syncretic elements.

21. The ideas in this section reflect many years of conversation with David Brown. Our mutual interests in the practice of Santería, his support, and his active engagement in my thinking have made this section possible. As the young Cubans say, for me he is *mortal.*

22. This idea has had enormous play in the cultures where European philosophy has had a significant impact. Although the history of this idea is beyond the scope of this work, it is important to note three key issues. One model of presence comes from Descartes, for whom the subject was unitary, ahistorical, and the grounding entity for rational thought. Another model comes from Hume, for whom the subject was a sensing experiencer of the empirical world. In recent years, deconstructionists such as Derrida and feminists such as Spivak and Kristeva have called these notions into question through philosophy's own discourse and through cross-cultural comparison. See the conclusion for a fuller discussion of these issues.

23. *Invocation* and *incarnation* have been used by a variety of students of Yoruba expressive culture to explore its relationship to the potent and determining otherworld. See Thompson 1983:3–5; Drewal, Pemberton, and Abiodun 1989; Drewal 1992; and Abiodun, Drewal, and Pemberton 1994.

24. Hardin also argues that people are aesthetic in the production and evaluation of practice—an insight that has relevance to the political aspects of ritual.

25. This statement, quoted by Hardin (1993:13) reflects the powerful if seldom cited influence of Berger and Luckmann's *Social Construction of Reality* (1966), in which they argue for an almost identical understanding of the processes of social production and reproduction.

26. Barber has made this point convincingly for the Yoruba, who say that "the orisha's power and splendour depend on its having numerous attentive (and wealthy) devotees to glorify its name" (1981:725). Neither this statement nor my own formulation implies that the divinities do not exist without human action, only that their presence is less noticeable without that action.

27. Though it is counter to the overall argument of this chapter, Bloch's insights (1992) into the almost universal religious processes and the "core" ritual structure of "rebounding violence" apply to the asiento. He argues that vitality is taken from sacrificed animals through violence, and this vitality is then transferred to humans for their transformation. This universal structure results from universal human constraints and is mitigated by historically constituted political concerns (1992:3–4).

28. The asientos of Changó, Obatalá, Ochún, and Yemayá are considered simple because they are the most frequently performed and require the fewest number of extra ceremonies. The initiations of Elegguá, Ogún, Ochosi, and Oyá are famous for their difficulty.

29. Oríaté Ernesto Pichardo says that this tradition is mistaken: in his view, the secret of the river should go into Ochún's sacred container or into the container in which water is brought back from the river. Very knowledgeable practitioners say the stone is the sacred manifestation of the first person initiated, Ibá Omí.

30. William Bascom (1980) produced the most scholarly text on this subject, but many santeros have written manuals explaining the process of divining with the cowries. See Angarica 1955; Cortéz n.d.; Ecún 1988; and Elizondo n.d.

31. This contrast between cool and hot can be seen in other areas of religious practice as well. Orichas themselves are sometimes described as cool or hot to mean either gentle or aggressive.

32. This explanation, which sounds remarkably like those put forth by Yoruba orisha worshipers (Drewal 1992:30–32, 51–52, 56, 78–79), usually comes from sophisticated and well-trained practitioners who have been working with the asiento ritual for many years. It is interesting to note that in the most traditional oricha houses newborn children are washed in omiero.

33. Most orichas "take" water, although Babalú-Ayé "takes" dry wine and the liquid from inside fresh coconuts.

34. This Caribbean rodent is larger than a rat and smaller than a possum. It is sometimes called "nutria" in English.

35. These ingredients are commonly added to herbs and water to direct the aché within the omiero in specific ways. Each of these medicines adds its aché to the overall mixture.

36. Santeros frequently repeat, *"Sin Osain, no hay santo"* (Sp. without Osain there is no oricha) to recall the important role this oricha plays in the asiento and all aspects of the religion.

37. *Bledo blanco* is called *lobé* in Lucumí and slender amaranth in English; its binomial is *Amaranthus viridis* (Cabrera 1983:346). *Peregún* is called *cordobán* in Spanish and

Moses-in-the-cradle in English; its binomial is *Rholo discolar* (Cabrera 1983:410). *Wereyeye* is called *peonía* in Spanish and peony in English; its binomial is *Arbus precatorius* (Cabrera 1983:514). There is not always agreement, even among knowledgeable practitioners, about which herbs should be used. See J. Mason 1985:64–65 for additional information.

38. See Brandon 1990, Ecún 1985, and J. Mason 1985 for detailed descriptions of the process of sacrifice.

39. This quotation comes from an oríaté in Washington, D.C., who was sacrificing a goat to Ochún in November 1993.

40. See, for example, Buckley 1985:140–165. It is also interesting to note that these praise songs function much as *oriki* do in Yoruba culture; see Barber 1991:10–38.

41. Matory has done an impressive catalogue and analysis of the tropes at play in the possession religion of the Yoruba and in their initiation rites; see Matory 1994:170–215.

42. See Pérez Medina and Herrera Hernández 1995:28. Ernesto Pichardo explains that the entire asiento reenacts the movement of the soul from heaven to earth; he correlates each ceremony in the asiento to an event in the soul's migration and thus insists that the trope of rebirth should be central to any interpretation of the asiento as a whole.

43. Children of Obatalá have completely white *trajes del almuerzo*.

44. These implements are many and beyond the scope of this argument. At the most basic level, Ochún and Yemayá carry fans, Changó carries a double-headed ax, and Obatalá carries a cane. These objects are often covered in cloth or elaborately beaded.

45. This language and ritual imagery also include equestrian metaphors. These images of horse and rider are less prevalent in the Regla de Ocha than in Yoruba or Haitian rites. See Deren 1970 and Matory 1994.

46. Several priestesses I know have reported a similar dream following their asientos: In their dreams, these priestesses are being sacrificed to their head-ruling orichas. These dreams, though different in their details, include the same self-sacrifice motifs present in the asiento.

47. Note that Matory (1994:10–11) explains that the king of Oyo's wives were called "iyawó" and were named using the praise-names of the king.

48. See D. Brown 1996 for an example of how this understanding translates into social and artistic action.

49. I have not presented the parental tropes that also run throughout discourse about the orichas because this set of images is not as central to the asiento.

50. Similarly, all the orichas need a corps of active priests to praise and worship them if they are to have more followers in the future. Some practitioners claim that the orichas' need for followers encourages them to fulfill the requests of their priests.

5. IMAGINING POWER: *The Aesthetics of Aché in Santería*

1. In this first section of this chapter, I have used pseudonyms to protect the privacy of those involved.

2. Practitioners of the religion often use simple explanations like this one when they are asked to describe the orichas. These phrases are meant to convey the essence of the divinities but also to maintain a certain mystery and secrecy.

3. To "make an oricha" is to initiate or be initiated into the worship of a particular divinity. With this ceremony a practitioner can begin to act as an intermediary between people and the orichas.

4. See Thompson 1983:5–16 for a longer, transatlantic, and idealized discussion of the concept; see Drewal 1992 for several important discussions of aché in Yoruba culture and performance.

5. In this model syncretism is a historical process in which two religions or cultures merge into one unified complex; see Droogers 1988.

6. Practitioners use Lucumí words for sacrifice and ritual that allude to worship. The Spanish verb *adorar* (adore, worship) is rarely if ever used to describe the religious practices of the religion, although the noun *culto* (worship) is used for the whole religious system.

7. I recently started to undertake oral historical and archival research on the history of the tradition, and the emergent findings confirm what Rafael López Valdés and David Brown have been saying.

8. I would like to thank Ernesto Pichardo for pointing this out to me.

9. By *action* I mean nothing more than intentional behavior.

10. James opened the philosophical territory that we are now mapping with ethnographic research. In *Essays in Radical Empiricism* (1976), he argued that all experience was organized by the "selective interest" and "selective activity" of the experiencer. Through selection and attention, the experiencer creates a lifeworld of lived experience—"our living realities" (1950, vol. 2: 295).

11. In the hermeneutical circle of the social construction of reality, individuals and groups encounter the world in a particular form, engage and work upon that world, and then are faced with the results of their labor, a transformed objective world. The social imaginary is at the very least one aspect of that hermeneutic and plays a cyclical role in the process of social and symbolic actions, although many authors argue for the primacy of the image or structure in the process (see Maffesoli 1993b; Tacussel 1993).

12. Much research has been done on this subject in recent years. For an excellent example of the use and power of metaphoric images in Yoruba culture, see Matory 1993:58–85.

13. See Matory 1993:82 for one methodology for working on tropes within a cultural complex. See also Durand 1993 for a theoretical and methodological statement on the social imaginary. Those working on the social imaginary—especially Maffesoli—harbor a deep and abiding interest in the everyday as well. In 1989 Maffesoli edited a special issue of *Current Sociology* (vol. 37, no. 1) that addressed the sociology of everyday life; one of the contributors was Thomas Luckmann who helped revive constructionist social theories.

14. Pichardo is most famous for his Church of the Lukumí Babalú-Ayé, which has drawn much attention from other practitioners and the larger public. Through a bitter struggle with municipal officials in Hialeah, Florida, the church won a case before the United States Supreme Court, granting the right to practice all traditional aspects to the Regla de Ocha, including animal sacrifice.

15. The Lucumí word *italero* describes the ritual specialist who orchestrates large ceremonies and performs important divination sessions, especially those associated with the initiation of new priestesses and priests. Many people use it interchangeably with *oríaté*.

16. I have tried to reproduce the dialogue that we had from the notes that I made. In turn I have given the text to Pichardo to be certain that it accurately reflects his views. In this section, I have spelled Lucumí words in a more Yoruba way, just as Pichardo pronounces them. For example, the Lucumí *aché* originated from the Yoruba *àshé,* and because of his desire to focus on the African legacy of the religion, Pichardo approxi-

mates this pronunciation. I have transcribed it as he actually says it with a stress on the last syllable; similarly, he often says *orisha* instead of *oricha*.

17. This monologue represents one perspective from a very knowledgeable and respected ritual specialist. It is also included to communicate to the reader the fractured and provisional quality of the information garnered through fieldwork and from which we create our knowledge of other cultures (see Dwyer 1982:255–286).

18. This invocation is used again and again in the religion and defines its major motives and values. The idea and image of resolve (Sp. *la firmeza*) permeates much of the religious discourse of the Regla de Ocha; it is an area that deserves more investigation in the future. There are variations of this invocation; the one given here is used in the ritual house in Cuba where I work. The famous babalawo Enrique Hernández of Guanabacoa, Cuba, prays for "health, luck, strength, and the conquest of all difficulties" (Sp. *la salud, la suerte, la fuerza, y el vencimiento de todas las dificultades*).

19. This phrase is commonly used when people describe Yemayá. I first heard it from José Velázquez in the summer of 1990.

20. See M. Mason 1992 for description and interpretation of dilogún divination, including a transcription of a full divination session performed by a Cuban-American priest of Obatalá.

21. A technical vocabulary designates the different instruments used to facilitate the calling and descent of the gods. A *tambor* (Sp. lit. drum, drumming) includes those performances where the percussion is produced by the sacred *batá* drums. A *güiro* (Sp. lit. gourd, a gourd rattle with a beaded net) uses a conga drum, several rattles, and a *hierro* (Sp. lit. iron, a hoe blade or other piece of metal struck with a stick). Both of these performances can also be dedicated to the dead, and both can be called a *toque* (Sp. playing). Any of these can be considered ebó.

22. In the vast literature on Yoruba culture, these domains consistently exist in dynamic and mutually defining opposition. See Drewal (1992:26) and McClelland (1982:33). Interestingly Awolalu (1979:58) translates *òrun* as "hereafter." Although this treatment reflects his Christian apologetics generally, this domain—as understood both by the Yoruba and those who practice the Regla de Ocha—does include the spirits of the deceased while at the same time not being defined by that fact. However, Drewal (1992: xv) states that Yorubas use the word *heaven* to translate *òrun*. Because most practitioners I have worked with refer to heaven as the abode of Olodumare, the High God, and the spirits of the dead, and because *orun* (Lu.) contains much more than these agents, I have employed *spiritual world* because it has less conceptual baggage for my readers.

23. This scheme comes from Murphy 1981.

24. This is the plural of *ebó*. The Spanish plural marker *ces* is added to the Lucumí root.

25. See D. Brown 1989 for an extended discussion of these situations and how they are negotiated.

26. This odu is called Obara-Ogbe in Ifá divination. Most of the odus have the same names, but the differences confound people and create conflicts when they work with both dilogún divination and Ifá. In fact, no consensus exists regarding the correspondences between the odus in the two systems.

27. The whole series of divination signs that come out in an itá can lead a person to a close relationship with a deity other than the head-ruling oricha. In 1996 a priest of Yemayá told me that in his itá, all five odus included Obara, a sign where Changó—the regal

oricha of thunder—asserts himself forcefully. The priest said, "It's 'I give thanks to Changó' every day with me."

28. See D. Brown 1989 for an excellent discussion of the contestations that occur between the babalawos and the italeros.

29. Note, though, that the pursuit of status does not qualify as an "interest" and is therefore not incompatible with the "good heart."

30. Ethnographer Adrienne Kaeppler has said that all serious anthropologists must, to some extent, enter the world of the cultures they study (personal communication, August 1997).

6. SANTERÍA AND THE SOCIAL CONSTRUCTION OF SUBJECTIVITY

1. This statement applies with equal accuracy to the formalized initiations of the Regla de Ocha and to the less clearly marked initiatory phases in the local practices of European Spiritism, which most Santería priests also practice.

2. Before receiving the Warriors, most neophytes first receive the necklaces of the orichas. In this ceremony, a priestess usually consecrates a set of color-coded, beaded necklaces to the central orichas Elegguá, Ochún, Yemayá, Changó, and Obatalá; in some houses, Oyá's necklace is also included (see D. Brown 1989:403). These are presented to the head of the neophyte and placed around the neck. This act connects the neophyte's spiritual essence to the priestess's orichas. In one interpretation, this initiation binds the neophyte to that particular religious house, although in practice these connections are often severed for various reasons. Others claim that the necklaces connect the neophyte only to the orichas.

3. Women are excluded almost entirely from the rituals of the priests of Orula called *babalawos*. Similarly, in the Havana-based lineages (Sp. *ramas*) of the religion, all priestesses and priests must undergo a special initiation called *cuchillo* (Sp. knife) before they can sacrifice four-legged animals. Some babalawos insist that this right is theirs alone and claim that the ceremony of cuchillo is an invention.

4. I am grateful to Ivan Karp for helping me begin to think through these ideas.

5. This developmental differentiation of subjectivity in the religion resembles the changes in personhood throughout the life cycle, as described in the literature. See Whittaker 1992 for a good introduction.

6. Efuché, the famous religious reformer of the nineteenth century, officiated at many ceremonies and effectively transformed various ritual structures through her knowledge and charisma. Timotea Albeal, known as Latwán in the religion, was the leading oríaté in Havana from the beginning of the twentieth century until her death in 1935 (de León 1997). In contemporary Miami, a religious elder in her fifties is emerging as an oríaté (Pichardo 2001).

7. The phrase "by my sign" (Sp. *por mi signo*) represents the most common element in these justifications.

8. This secrecy has had some nefarious applications as well. Some practitioners have traveled to Cuba and returned to the United States claiming to have undergone important initiations. Without social contact between the two sides, these initiations are often difficult to verify. Secrecy always allows for the possibility of betrayal, a highly charged concept in the Santería religion and in Cuban society.

9. It is common to hear practitioners discuss the impact of other people's emotions on them and their clients. Envy is thought to be a particularly powerful force of ruin.

REFERENCES

Abiodun, Rowland, Henry Drewal, and John Pemberton. 1994. *The Yoruba Artist: New Theoretical Perspectives on African Arts*. Washington, D.C.: Smithsonian Institution Press.

Abrahams, Roger. 1977. "Toward an Enactment-Centered Theory of Folklore." In W. Bascom, ed., *Frontiers of Folklore*, pp. 79–120. Boulder: Westview Press.

———. 1986a. "Pragmatism and a Folklore of Experience." *Western Folklore* 44:324–332.

———. 1986b. "Ordinary and Extraordinary Experience." In V. Turner and E. Bruner, eds., *The Anthropology of Experience*, pp. 45–72. Urbana: University of Illinois Press.

Alcoff, Linda. 1988. "Cultural Feminism versus Post-Structuralism: The Identity Crisis in Feminist Theory." *Signs* 13:405–436.

Angarica, Nicolas. 1955. *Manual de orihate: Religión lucumí*. Havana: n.p.

Apter, Andrew. 1992. *Black Critics and Kings: The Hermeneutics of Power in Yoruba Society*. Chicago: University of Chicago Press.

Arens, W., and Ivan Karp. 1989. "Introduction." In W. Arens and I. Karp, eds., *Creativity of Power: Cosmology and Action in African Societies*, pp. xi–xxix. Washington, D.C.: Smithsonian Institution Press.

Argüelles Mederos, Anibal, and Ileana Hodge Limonta. 1991. *Los llamados cultos sincréticos y espiritismo: Estudio monográfico sobre su significación social en la sociedad cubana*. Havana: Editorial Academia.

Armstrong, Robert Plant. 1971. *The Affecting Presence: An Essay in Humanistic Anthropology*. Urbana: University of Illinois Press.

———. 1981. *The Powers of Presence: Consciousness, Myth, and Affecting Presence*. Philadelphia: University of Pennsylvania Press.

Awolalu, J. Omosade. 1979. *Yoruba Beliefs and Sacrificial Rites*. London: Longman Group.

Babcock, Barbara. 1980. "Reflexivity: Definitions and Discriminations." *Semiotica* 30 (1/2): 1–14.

Bakhtin, Mikhail. 1981. *The Dialogical Imagination*. M. Holquist, ed. Austin: University of Texas Press.

Barber, Karin. 1981. "How Man Makes God in West Africa: Yoruba Attitudes towards Orisa." *Africa* 51:724–745.
———. 1991. *I Could Speak until Tomorrow: Oriki, Women, and the Past in a Yoruba Town.* Washington, D.C.: Smithsonian Institution Press.
Bascom, William. 1944. "The Sociological Role of the Yoruba Cult Group." *American Anthropologist*, n.s. 46 (no. 1, pt. 2, Memoirs 63): 1–75.
———. 1965. "Four Functions of Folklore." In A. Dundes, ed., *The Study of Folklore*, pp. 279–298. Englewood Cliffs, N.J.: Prentice-Hall.
———. 1980. *Sixteen Cowries.* Bloomington: Indiana University Press.
———. 1991. *Ifá Divination: Communication between Gods and Men in West Africa.* Bloomington: Indiana University Press.
Bastide, Roger. 1978. *The African Religions of Brazil: Toward a Sociology of the Interpenetrations of Civilizations.* (Originally published 1960.) Baltimore: Johns Hopkins University Press.
Bauman, Richard. 1972. "Differential Identity and the Social Base of Folklore." In A. Paredes and R. Bauman, eds., *Toward New Perspectives in Folklore*, pp. 31–41. Austin: University of Texas Press.
———. 1977. *Verbal Art as Performance.* Prospect Heights, Ill.: Waveland Press.
———. 1983. "The Field Study of Folklore in Context." In R. Dorson, ed., *The Handbook of American Folklore*, pp. 362–368. Bloomington: Indiana University Press.
———. 1986. *Story, Performance, and Event: Contextual Studies of Oral Narrative.* Cambridge: Cambridge University Press.
———. 1989. "Performance." In E. Barouw, ed., *International Encyclopedia of Communications*, vol. 3, pp. 262–266. New York: Oxford University Press.
———. 1992. "Contextualization, Tradition, and the Dialogue of Genres: Icelandic Legends of the *Krafaskáld.*" In C. Goodwin and A. Duranti, eds., *Rethinking Context*, pp. 125–145. Cambridge: Cambridge University Press.
Bauman, Richard, and Charles Briggs. 1990. "Poetics and Performance as Critical Perspectives on Language and Social Life." *Annual Review of Anthropology* 19:59–88.
Beidelman, T. O. 1986. *Moral Imagination in Kaguru Modes of Thought.* Bloomington: Indiana University Press.
Benedict, Ruth. 1935. *Zuni Mythology.* New York: Columbia University Press.
Berger, Peter, and Thomas Luckmann. 1966. *The Social Construction of Reality: A Treatise in the Sociology of Knowledge.* New York: Anchor Books.
Bloch, Maurice. 1992. *Prey into Hunter: The Politics of Religious Experience.* Cambridge: Cambridge University Press.
Blumer, Herbert. 1969. *Symbolic Interactionism: Perspective and Method.* Englewood Cliffs, N.J.: Prentice-Hall.
Bourdieu, Pierre. 1989. *Outline of a Theory of Practice.* (Originally published 1977.) Cambridge: Cambridge University Press.
Brandon, George. 1983. *The Dead Sell Memories.* Ann Arbor: University Microfilms International.
———. 1990. "Sacrificial Practices in Santería, an African-Cuban Religion in the United States." In J. Holloway, ed., *Africanisms in American Culture*, pp. 119–148. Bloomington: Indiana University Press.

———. 1993. *Santería from Africa to the New World: The Dead Sell Memories*. Bloomington: Indiana University Press.

Bravos Pineda, Raquel. 1993. Interview with the author, Washington, D.C., 14 October.

Brown, David. 1989. Garden in the Machine: Afro-Cuban Sacred Art and Performance in Urban New Jersey and New York. Ph.D. dissertation, Yale University.

———. 1993. "Thrones of the Orichas: Afro-Cuban Altars in New Jersey, New York, and Havana." *African Arts* 26 (4): 44–59, 85–87.

———. 1995. Ritual Genealogies of Ifá in Cuba and the United States. Paper given at the Latin American Studies Association meeting, Washington, D.C., 19 September.

———. 1996. "Toward an Ethnoaesthetics of Santería Ritual Arts: The Practice of Altar-Making and Gift Exchange." In A. Lindsay, ed., *Santería Aesthetics in Contemporary Latin American Art*, pp. 77–146. Washington, D.C.: Smithsonian Institution Press.

———. 2003. *Thrones of the Orichas: Art, Ritual, and Innovation in Afro-Cuban Santería*. Chicago: University of Chicago Press.

Brown, Karen M. 1991. *Mama Lola: A Vodou Priestess in Brooklyn*. Berkeley: University of California Press.

Bruner, Edward. 1986. "Experience and Its Expression." In V. Turner and E. Bruner, eds., *The Anthropology of Experience*, pp. 3–30. Urbana: University of Illinois Press.

Buckley, Anthony. 1985. *Yoruba Medicine*. Oxford: Clarendon Press.

Cabrera, Lydia. 1977. *La Regla Kimbisa de Santo Cristo del Buen Viaje*. Miami: Colección del Chicherekú en el exilio.

———. 1980. *Yemayá y Ochún*. Miami: Colección del Chicherekú en el exilio.

———. 1983. *El monte (Igbo-Finda; Ewe Orisha; Vititi Nfinda)*. Miami: Colección del Chicherekú.

Carter, George. 1990. Telephone interview with the author, Bloomington, Ind., and Washington, D.C., 7 December.

Clifford, James. 1988. *The Predicament of Culture: Twentieth Century Ethnography, Literature, and Art*. Cambridge, Mass.: Harvard University Press.

Comaroff, Jean. 1985. *Body of Power, Spirit of Resistance*. Chicago: University of Chicago Press.

Comaroff, Jean, and John Comaroff. 1993. "Introduction." In J. Comaroff and J. Comaroff, eds., *Modernity and Its Malcontents: Ritual and Power in Postcolonial Africa*, pp. xi–xxxvii. Chicago: University of Chicago Press.

Cortéz, Enrique. n.d. *Manual del italero de la religión yoruba*. n.p.: n.p.

Cowan, Jane. 1990. *Dance and the Body Politic in Northern Greece*. Princeton: Princeton University Press.

Crapanzano, Vincent. 1977. "On the Writing of Ethnography." *Dialectical Anthropology* 2:69–73.

———. 1980. *Tuhami, Portrait of a Moroccan*. Chicago: University of Chicago Press.

———. 1992. *Hermes' Dilemma and Hamlet's Desire: On the Epistemology of Interpretation*. Cambridge, Mass.: Harvard University Press.

Csikszentmihaly, Mihaly, and Rick E. Robinson. 1990. *The Art of Seeing: An Interpretation of the Aesthetic Encounter*. Malibu, Calif.: J. P. Getty Trust and the Getty Center for Education in the Arts.

Daniel, E. Valentine. 1984. *Fluid Signs: Being a Person the Tamil Way*. Berkeley: University of California Press.

Deiterlen, G., ed. 1973. *La notion de personne en Afrique noire*. Paris: Editions du Centre National de la Recherche Scientifique.

de León, Angel. 1997. Interview with the author, Havana, 3 August.

Deren, Maya. 1970. *Divine Horsemen: Voodoo Gods of Haiti*. New York: Chelsea House.

Devereux, George. 1967. *From Anxiety to Method in the Behavioural Sciences*. The Hague: Mouton.

Dewey, John. 1934. *Art As Experience*. New York: Capricorn Books.

Dolby-Stahl, Sandra. 1977. "The Personal Narrative as Folklore." *Journal of the Folklore Institute* 14:9–30.

———. 1989. *Literary Folkloristics and the Personal Narrative*. Bloomington: Indiana University Press.

Domínguez, Virginia. 1991. "How the Self Stacks the Deck." *Anthropology and Humanism Quarterly* 16:12–15.

Douglas, Mary. 1978. *Implicit Meanings: Essays in Anthropology*. London: Routledge & Kegan Paul.

Drewal, Henry, John Pemberton, and Roland Abiodun. 1989. *Yoruba: Nine Centuries of African Art and Thought*. New York: Center for African Art / Harry N. Abrams.

Drewal, Margaret. 1992. *Yoruba Ritual: Performers, Play, Agency*. Bloomington: Indiana University Press.

Droogers, Andre. 1988. "Syncretism: The Problem of Definition, the Definition of the Problem." In J. Gort, ed., *Dialogue and Syncretism: An Interdisciplinary Approach*, pp. 7–25. Grand Rapids, Mich.: W. B. Eerdmans.

Dundes, Alan. 1980. *Interpreting Folklore*. Bloomington: Indiana University Press.

Durand, Gilbert. 1993. "The Implications of the Imaginary and Societies." *Current Sociology* 41 (2): 17–32.

Durkheim, Emile. 1954. *The Elementary Forms of the Religious Life*. (Originally published 1911.) London: Allen and Unwin.

Dwyer, Kevin. 1982. *Moroccan Dialogues: Anthropology in Question*. Baltimore: Johns Hopkins University Press.

Ecún, Obá. 1985. *Oricha: Metodología de la religión yoruba*. Miami: Editorial SIBI.

———. 1988. *Addimú: Ofrenda a los orichas*. Miami: Editorial SIBI.

Ekman, Paul. 1977. "Biological and Cultural Contributions to Body and Facial Movement." In J. Blacking, ed., *Anthropology of the Body*, pp. 39–84. New York: Academic Press.

Elizondo, Carlos. n.d. *Manual del italero de la religión lucumí*. Union City, N.J.: n.p.

Elster, John. 1986. "Introduction." In J. Elster, ed., *The Multiple Self*, pp. 1–34. Cambridge: Cambridge University Press.

Fabian, J. 1983. *Time and the Other: How Anthropology Makes Its Object*. New York: Columbia University Press.

Fagg, William. 1973. "In Search of Meaning in African Art." In A. Forge, ed., *Primitive Art and Society*, pp. 151–168. London: Oxford University Press.

Feher, Michel. 1989. "Introduction to Fragments of a History of the Human Body." *Zone* 3:10–17.

Fernandez, James. 1982. *Bwiti*. Princeton: Princeton University Press.

———. 1986. "The Argument of Images and the Experience of Returning to the Whole." In

V. Turner and E. Bruner, eds., *The Anthropology of Experience*, pp. 159–187. Urbana: University of Illinois Press.

———. 1991. "Introduction: Confluents of Inquiry." In J. Fernandez, ed., *Beyond Metaphor: The Theory of Tropes in Anthropology*, pp. 1–13. Stanford: Stanford University Press.

Fitzgerald, Dale. 1975. "The Language of Ritual Events among the Ga of Southern Ghana." In B. Blount and M. Sanches, eds., *Sociolinguistic Dimensions of Language Uses*, pp. 205–234. New York: Academic Press.

Flores, Ysamur. 1990. "Fit for the Queen: A Consecration Outfit for Yemayá." *Folklore Forum* 23:47–56.

Flores, Ysamur, and Robin Evanchuk. 1994. *Santería Garments and Altars: Speaking Without a Voice*. Jackson: University Press of Mississippi.

Fortes, Meyer. 1973. "On the Concept of the Person among the Tallensi." In G. Deiterlen, ed., *La notion de personne en Afrique noire*, pp. 283–319. Paris: Editions de Centre National de la Recherche Scientifique.

Foucault, Michel. 1977. "What Is an Author?" In D. Bouchard, ed., *Language, Counter-Memory, Practice: Selected Essays and Interviews by Michel Foucault*, pp. 113–138. Ithaca, N.Y.: Cornell University Press.

Friedman, Robert. 1982. Making an Abstract World Concrete: Knowledge, Competence, and Structural Dimensions of Performance among Batá Drummers in Santería. Ph.D. dissertation, Indiana University.

Galeano, Eduardo. 1991. *The Book of Embraces*. New York: W. W. Norton.

Geertz, Clifford. 1973. *The Interpretation of Cultures*. New York: Basic Books.

———. 1983. *Local Knowledge: Further Essays in Interpretive Anthropology*. New York: Basic Books.

Giddens, Anthony. 1979. *Central Problems in Social Theory: Action, Structure and Contradiction in Social Analysis*. Berkeley: University of California Press.

———. 1993. *New Rules of Sociological Method: A Positive Critique of Interpretive Sociologies*. Cambridge: Polity Press.

Gilroy, Paul. 1993. *The Black Atlantic: Double Consciousness and Modernity*. Cambridge, Mass.: Harvard University Press.

Glassner, Barry. 1990. "Fit for Postmodern Selfhood." In H. Becker and M. McCall, eds., *Symbolic Interaction and Cultural Studies*, pp. 215–243. Chicago: University of Chicago Press.

Gleason, Judith. 1987. *Oyá: In Praise of the Goddess*. Boston: Shambhala.

Goffman, Erving. 1959. *The Presentation of Self in Everyday Life*. Garden City, N.Y.: Doubleday.

———. 1974. *Frame Analysis: An Essay on the Organization of Experience*. New York: Harper & Row.

González, P. 1992. Interview with the author, Hyattsville, Md., 13 December.

González-Wippler, Migene. 1985. *Introduction to Seashell Divination*. New York: Original Publications.

———. 1989. *Santería: The Religion*. New York: Harmony Books.

Greenblatt, Stephan. 1980. *Renaissance Self-Fashioning: From More to Shakespeare*. Chicago: University of Chicago Press.

Gregory, S. 1986. *Santería in New York City*. Ann Arbor: University Microfilms International.

Hagedorn, Katherine. 1995. *Anatomía del Proceso Folklórico:* The "Folkloricization" of Afro-Cuban Religious Performance in Cuba. Ph.D. dissertation, Brown University.

———. 2000. "Bringing down the Santo: An Analysis of Possession Performance in Afro-Cuban Santería." *The World of Music* 42 (2): 99–113.

———. 2001. *Divine Utterances: The Performance of Afro-Cuban Santería.* Washington, D.C.: Smithsonian Institution Press.

Handler, Richard, and Jocelyn Linnekin. 1984. "Tradition, Genuine or Spurious." *Journal of American Folklore* 97:273–290.

Hanks, William. 1984. "Sanctification, Structure, and Experience in a Yucatec Ritual Event." *Journal of American Folklore* 97:131–166.

Hardin, Kris. 1993. *The Aesthetics of Action: Continuity and Change in a West African Town.* Washington, D.C.: Smithsonian Institution Press.

Hastrup, Kirsten. 1992. "Writing Ethnography: State of the Art." In J. Okely and H. Callaway, eds., *Anthropology and Autobiography,* pp. 116–133. New York: Routledge.

Herdt, Gilbert. 1990. "Secret Societies and Secret Collectives." *Oceania* 60:360–381.

Hernández, María. 1991. Telephone interview with the author, Washington, D.C., and Albuquerque, N.M., 15 May.

Hillman, James. 1992. *Re-Visioning Psychology.* New York: Harper Perennial.

Hobsbawm, Eric, and Terence Ranger, eds. 1983. *The Invention of Tradition.* Cambridge: Cambridge University Press.

Horton, Robin. 1983. "Social Psychologies: African and Western." In M. Fortes, *Oedipus and Job in West African Religion,* pp. 41–82. Cambridge: Cambridge University Press.

Hymes, Dell. 1974. *Foundations in Sociolinguistics: An Ethnographic Approach.* Philadelphia: University of Pennsylvania Press.

———. 1975. "Folklore's Nature and the Sun's Myth." *Journal of American Folklore* 88:345–369.

Jackson, Michael. 1986. *Barawa or the Way the Birds Fly.* Washington, D.C.: Smithsonian Institution Press.

———. 1989. *Paths toward a Clearing: Radical Empiricism and Ethnographic Inquiry.* Bloomington: Indiana University Press.

———, ed. 1996. *Things as They Are: New Directions in Phenomenological Anthropology.* Bloomington: Indiana University Press.

Jackson, Michael, and Ivan Karp. 1990. "Introduction." In M. Jackson and I. Karp, eds., *Personhood and Agency: The Experience of Self and Other in African Cultures,* pp. 15–30. Uppsala: Acta Universitatis Upsaliensis.

Jacobson-Widding, Anita. 1990. "The Shadow as an Expression of Individuality in Congolese Concepts of Personhood." In M. Jackson and I. Karp, eds., *Personhood and Agency: The Experience of Self and Other in African Cultures,* pp. 31–58. Uppsala: Acta Universitatis Upsaliensis.

James, William. 1950. *The Principles of Psychology.* (Originally published 1890.) New York: Dover Press.

———. 1976. *Essays in Radical Empiricism.* (Originally published 1912.) Cambridge, Mass.: Harvard University Press.

———. 1978. *Pragmatism.* (Originally published 1907.) Cambridge, Mass.: Harvard University Press.

Kapferer, Bruce. 1986. "Performance and the Structuring of Meaning and Experience." In

V. Turner and E. Bruner, eds., *The Anthropology of Experience*, pp. 188–203. Urbana: University of Illinois Press.

Karp, Ivan. 1986. "Agency and Social Theory: A Review of Anthony Giddens." *American Ethnologist* 13:131–137.

———. 1990. "Power and Capacity in Iteso Rituals of Possession." In M. Jackson and I. Karp, eds., *Personhood and Agency*, pp. 79–94. Uppsala: Acta Universitatis Upsaliensis.

Karp, Ivan, and Martha Kendall. 1982. "Reflexivity in Fieldwork." In P. Secord, ed., *Explaining Human Behavior*, pp. 249–273. Los Angeles: Sage Publications.

Karp, Ivan, and Kent Maynard. 1983. "Reading the Nuer." *Current Anthropology* 24 (4): 481–503.

Keller, Catherine. 1986. *From a Broken Web: Separation, Sexism, and Self*. Boston: Beacon Press.

Lacan, Jacques. 1978. *Ecríts: A Selection*. A. Sheridan, trans. New York: W. W. Norton.

Lakoff, George, and Mark Johnson. 1980. *Metaphors We Live By*. Chicago: University of Chicago Press.

Leavitt, John. 1996. "Meaning and Feeling in the Anthropology of Emotions." *American Ethnologist* 23:514–539.

Leder, Drew. 1990. *The Absent Body*. Chicago: University of Chicago Press.

Lévi-Strauss, Claude. 1979. "The Effectiveness of Symbols." In W. Lessa and E. Vogt, eds., *The Comparative Reader in Religion*, pp. 318–327. New York: Harper & Row.

Lienhardt, Godfrey. 1961. *Divinity and Experience: The Religion of the Dinka*. Oxford: Oxford University Press.

López Valdés, Rafael. 1985. *Componentes africanos en el etnos cubano*. Havana: Editorial de Ciencias Sociales.

———. 1995. Cabildos de africanos y religiones afrocubanas: Un nuevo enfoque. Unpublished manuscript.

Lukes, Steven. 1980. "Types of Individualism." In P. P. Wiener, ed., *Dictionary of the History of Ideas*, vol. 11, pp. 594–604. New York: Scribner.

Lutz, Catherine, and Geoffrey White. 1986. "The Anthropology of Emotions." *Annual Review of Anthropology* 16:405–436.

MacAloon, John. 1984a. "Introduction." In J. MacAloon, ed., *Rite, Drama, Festival, Spectacle: Rehearsals toward a Theory of Cultural Performances*, pp. 1–18. Philadelphia: Institute for the Study of Human Issues.

———. 1984b. "Olympic Games and the Theory of Spectacle in Modern Societies." In J. MacAloon, ed., *Rite, Drama, Festival, Spectacle: Rehearsals toward a Theory of Cultural Performances*, pp. 241–280. Philadelphia: Institute for the Study of Human Issues.

MacGaffey, Wyatt. 1990. "The Personhood of Ritual Objects: Kongo Minkisi." *Etnofoor* 3 (1): 45–61.

Maffesoli, Michel. 1985. *La connaissance ordinaire: Précis de sociologie compréhensive*. Paris: Librairie des Méridiens.

———. 1988. *Le temps des tribus: Le déclin de l'individualisme dans les sociétés masses*. Paris: Méridiens Klinksieck.

———. 1993a. "Introduction to Trend Report: The Social Imaginary." *Current Sociology* 41 (2): 1–6.

———. 1993b. "The Social Ambiance." *Current Sociology* 41 (2): 7–16.

——. 1993c. "The Imaginary and the Sacred in Durkheim's Sociology." *Current Sociology* 41 (2): 59–67.

Mamigliano, A. 1985. "Marcel Mauss and the Quest for the Person in Greek Biography and Autobiography." In M. Carrithers, S. Collins, and S. Lukes, eds., *The Category of the Person,* pp. 83–92. Cambridge: Cambridge University Press.

Marcel, Gabriel. 1962. *Homo Viator.* New York: Harper Torchbooks.

Marcus, George. 1991. "False Friends in a New Relationship: The Internal Critique of the Western Individual Self/Subject and Ethnographic Accounts of Other Selves." *Anthropology and Humanism Quarterly* 16:15–17.

Marcus, George, and Dick Cushman. 1982. "Ethnographies as Texts." *Annual Review of Anthropology* 11:25–69.

Marx, Karl. 1973. *Surveys from Exile.* (Originally published 1852.) Harmondsworth, England: Penguin.

Mason, John. 1985. *Four New World Yoruba Rituals.* Brooklyn: Yoruba Theological Archministry.

Mason, Michael Atwood. 1992. "The Blood That Runs in the Veins": Experience and Performance in Cuban-American *Santería* Divination. M.A. thesis, Indiana University.

——. 1993. "'The Blood That Runs in the Veins': The Creation of Identity and a Client's Experience of Cuban-American *Santería Dilogún* Divination." *Drama Review* 37 (2): 119–130.

——. 1994. "'I Bow My Head to the Ground': The Creation of Bodily Experience in a Cuban American *Santería* Initiation." *Journal of American Folklore* 107 (423): 23–39.

Matory, J. Lorand. 1993. "Government by Seduction: History and the Tropes of 'Mounting' in Oyo-Yoruba Religion." In J. Comaroff and J. Comaroff, eds., *Modernity and Its Malcontents: Ritual and Power in Postcolonial Africa,* pp. 58–85. Chicago: University of Chicago Press.

——. 1994. *Sex and the Empire That Is No More: Gender and the Politics of Metaphor in Oyo Yoruba Religion.* Minneapolis: University of Minnesota Press.

Mauss, Marcel. 1938. "Une catégorie de l'esprit humain: La notion de la personne, celle de «moi»." *Journal of the Royal Anthropological Institute* 68:263–282.

——. 1973. "Techniques of the Body." *Economy and Society* 2:70–88.

Mbiti, John. 1975. *Introduction to African Religion.* London: Heinemann Educational.

McArthur, Phillip. 1989. "Competence in Performance: A Critical Review." *Folklore Forum* 22:113–118.

McClelland, E. M. 1982. *The Cult of Ifá among the Yoruba,* vol. 1, *Folk Practice and the Art.* London: Ethnographica.

Mead, George Herbert. 1934. *Mind, Self, and Society.* Chicago: University of Chicago Press.

——. 1938. *The Philosophy of the Act.* Chicago: University of Chicago Press.

Minuchin, Salvador, Bernice Rosman, and Lester Baker. 1978. *Psychosomatic Families: Anorexia Nervosa in Context.* Cambridge, Mass.: Harvard University Press.

Morakinyo, Olufemi, and Akinsola Akiwowo. 1981. "The Yoruba Ontology of Personality and Motivation: A Multidisciplinary Approach." *Journal of Social and Biological Structures* 4 (1): 19–38.

Moreno Fraginales, Manuel. 1977. "Africa in Cuba: A Quantitative Analysis of the African Population in the Island of Cuba." *Annals of the New York Academy of Sciences* 292:187–201.

Mudimbe, V. Y. 1988. *The Invention of Africa: Gnosis, Philosophy, and the Order of Knowledge.* Bloomington: Indiana University Press.

Munn, Nancy. 1973. "Symbolism in a Ritual Context: Aspects of Symbolic Action." In J. Honigmann, ed., *The Handbook of Social and Cultural Anthropology,* pp. 579–612. Chicago: Rand McNally College Publishing.

Murphy, Joseph. 1981. Ritual Systems in Cuban Santería. Ph.D. dissertation, Temple University.

———. 1988. *Santería: An African Religion in America.* Boston: Beacon Press.

———. 1994. *Working the Spirit: Ceremonies of the African Diaspora.* Boston: Beacon Press.

Myerhoff, Barbara. 1984. "A Death in Due Time: Construction of Self and Culture in a Ritual Drama." In J. MacAloon, ed., *Rite, Drama, Festival, Spectacle: Rehearsals toward a Theory of Cultural Performances,* pp. 149–178. Philadelphia: Institute for the Study of Human Issues.

Nisbet, R. 1966. *The Sociological Tradition.* New York: Basic Books.

Obeyesekere, Gananath. 1990. *The Work of Culture: Symbolic Transformation in Psychoanalysis and Anthropology.* Chicago: University of Chicago Press.

Ogilvy, James. 1977. *Many Dimensional Man: Decentralizing Self, Society, and the Sacred.* New York: Oxford University Press.

Okely, Judith. 1992. "Anthropology and Autobiography: Participatory Experience and Embodied Knowledge." In J. Okely and H. Callaway, eds., *Anthropology and Autobiography,* pp. 1–28. London: Routledge.

Olmstead, David. 1953. "Comparative Notes on Yoruba and Lucumí." *Language* 29:157–164.

Ortega y Gasset, José. 1962. *Man and Crisis.* New York: W. W. Norton.

Ortiz, Fernando. 1984. "Los cabildos afrocubanos." (Originally published 1921.) In M. Barnet and A. Fernández, eds., *Ensayos etnográficos,* pp. 11–40. Havana: Editorial de Ciencias Sociales.

Ortner, Sherry. 1984. "Theory in Anthropology Since the Sixties." *Comparative Studies in Society and History* 26:126–166.

Palmié, Stephan. 1995. "Against Syncretism: 'Africanizing' and 'Cubanizing' Discourses in North American òrìsà Worship." In R. Fardon, ed., *Counterworks: Managing the Diversity of Knowledge,* pp. 73–104. New York: Routledge.

Pedraza-Bailey, Silvia. 1985. *Political and Economic Migrants in America: Cubans and Mexicans.* Austin: University of Texas Press.

Pérez Medina, Tomás, and Eloy Herrera Hernández. 1995. *El camino de Osha.* Caracas: Editorial Panapo.

Pichardo, Ernesto. 1994. Telephone interview with the author, Washington, D.C., and Miami, Fla., 15 December.

———. 2001. Interview with the author, Miami, Fla., 24 May.

Pile, Steve, and Nigel Thrift. 1995. "Introduction." In S. Pile and N. Thrift, eds., *Mapping the Subject: Geographies of Cultural Transformation,* pp. 1–12. London: Routledge.

Poole, Roger. 1975. "Objective Sign and Subjective Meaning." In J. Benthall and J. Polhemus, eds., *The Body as a Medium of Expression,* pp. 74–106. London: Allen Lane.

Ramos, Miguel "Willie." 1982. *Didá obí: Divinación através del coco.* Carolina, Puerto Rico: n.p.

———. 1996. "Afro-Cuban Orisha Worship." In A. Lindsay, ed., *Santería Aesthetics in Contemporary Latin American Art,* pp. 51–76. Washington, D.C.: Smithsonian Institution Press.

Rappaport, Roy. 1989. "Ritual." In E. Barnouw, ed., *International Encyclopedia of Communications,* vol. 3, pp. 467–473. New York: Oxford University Press.

Riesman, Paul. 1986. "The Person and the Life Cycle in African Social Life and Thought." *African Studies Review* 29 (2): 71–198.

Rogers, Andres. 1973. *Los caracoles.* Washington, D.C.: RICO Publishing.

Rorty, Richard. 1989. *Contingency, Irony, and Solidarity.* Cambridge: Cambridge University Press.

Rosaldo, Michelle. 1980. *Knowledge and Passion: Ilongot Notions of Self and Social Life.* New York: Cambridge University Press.

Rosaldo, Renato. 1984. "Grief and the Headhunter's Rage: On the Cultural Force of Emotions." In E. Bruner, ed., *Text, Play and Story,* pp. 178–195. Washington, D.C.: American Ethnological Society.

Sahlins, Marshall. 1981. *Historical Metaphors and Mythical Realities: Structure in the Early History of Sandwich Island Kingdoms.* Ann Arbor: University of Michigan Press.

Sánchez, Julio. 1978. *La religión de las orichas.* Hato Rey, Puerto Rico: n.p.

Sartre, Jean-Paul. 1969. "Itinerary of a Thought." *New Left Review* 58:43–66.

Schechner, Richard. 1985. *Between Theater and Anthropology.* Philadelphia: University of Pennsylvania Press.

Schechner, Richard, and Willa Appel, eds. 1990. *By Means of Performance: Intercultural Studies of Theatre and Ritual.* New York: Cambridge University Press.

Schieffelin, Edward. 1985. "Performance and the Cultural Construction of Reality." *American Ethnologist* 12:707–724.

Singer, Milton. 1984. *Man's Glassy Essence: Explorations in Semiotic Anthropology.* Bloomington: Indiana University Press.

Smith, Brewster. 1985. "The Metaphorical Basis of Selfhood." In A. Marsella, G. De Vos, and F. Hsu, eds., *Culture and Self: Asian and Western Perspectives,* pp. 56–88. London: Tavistock.

Spivak, Gayatri. 1990. *The Post-Colonial Critic: Interviews, Strategies, Dialogues.* New York: Routledge.

Stoeltje, Beverly. 1988. "Gender Representations in Performance: The Cowgirl and the Hostess." *Journal of Folklore Research* 25:141–153.

Stoeltje, Beverly, and Richard Bauman. 1989. "Community Festival and the Enactment of Modernity." In R. Walls and G. Schoemaker, eds., *The Old Traditional Way of Life: Essays in Honor of Warren Roberts,* pp. 159–171. Bloomington, Ind.: Trickster Press.

Tacussel, Patrick. 1993. "The Epistemological Propinquity of Social Aesthetics and the Imaginary." *Current Sociology* 41(2):33–42.

Thompson, Robert Farris. 1974. *African Art in Motion: Icon and Act.* Berkeley: University of California Press.

———. 1983. *Flash of the Spirit: African and Afro-American Art and Philosophy.* New York: Vintage Books.

Trinh, T. Minh-Ha. 1989. *Woman, Native, Other.* Bloomington: Indiana University Press.

Turner, Bryan. 1984. *The Body and Society.* Oxford: Basil Blackwell.

Turner, Victor. 1967. *The Forest of Symbols.* Ithaca, N.Y.: Cornell University Press.

————. 1969. *The Ritual Process: Structure and Anti-Structure*. Ithaca, N.Y.: Cornell University Press.

————. 1986. "Dewey, Dilthey, and Drama: An Essay in the Anthropology of Experience." In V. Turner and E. Bruner, eds., *The Anthropology of Experience*, pp. 33–44. Urbana: University of Illinois Press.

————. 1988. *The Anthropology of Performance*. New York: PAJ Publications.

Van Gennep, Arnold. 1909. *The Rites of Passage*. London: Routledge and Kegan Paul.

Velásquez, José. 1990a. Divination session with María Hernández taped by the author, Washington, D.C., 26 May.

————. 1990b. Interview with the author, Washington, D.C., 18 October.

Verger, Pierre Fatumbi. 1981. *Orixás: Deuses iorubás na África e no Novo Mundo*. São Paulo: Editora Corrupio Comércio.

Voloshinov, V. N. 1973. *Marxism and the Philosophy of Language*. New York: Seminar Press.

Wafer, Jim. 1991. *The Taste of Blood: Spirit Possession in Brazilian Candomblé*. Philadelphia: University of Pennsylvania Press.

Whittaker, Elvi. 1992. "The Birth of the Anthropological Self and Its Career." *Ethos* 20 (2): 191–219.

Williams, Raymond. 1973. "Base and Superstructure in Marxist Cultural Theory." *New Left Review* 82:3–16.

INDEX